P9-DNV-222

5ꞃ

B 73 : 42

BY THE SAME AUTHOR

A Cartoon History of Our Times

Low on the War

YEARS OF WRATH

A CARTOON HISTORY: 1931-1945

BY DAVID LOW

WITH A CHRONOLOGY AND TEXT
BY QUINCY HOWE

SIMON AND SCHUSTER • NEW YORK • 1946

ALL RIGHTS RESERVED INCLUDING THE RIGHT OF REPRODUCTION IN WHOLE OR IN PART

IN ANY FORM. COPYRIGHT, 1946, BY DAVID LOW. PUBLISHED BY SIMON AND SCHUSTER, INC.,

ROCKEFELLER CENTER, 1230 SIXTH AVENUE, NEW YORK 20, N. Y.

MANUFACTURED IN THE UNITED STATES OF AMERICA

PRINTED BY THE ACWELTONE CORP., NEW YORK

BOUND BY H. WOLFF BOOK MFG. CO., NEW YORK

PUBLISHER'S FOREWORD

The cartoons in this book span a fourteen-year period from September, 1931, to September, 1945. Nearly all of them first appeared in the London Evening Standard. *Approximately half of them have also been reproduced in two other collections of Mr. Low's work that we have published in the United States—his* Cartoon History of Our Times *which appeared in 1939 and* Low on the War *which appeared in 1941. The second of these two volumes brought the history of the war up to May 15, 1941. This collection not only covers the entire history of the war up to the surrender of Japan; it includes some early cartoons that did not appear in either of his other two books. News analyst Quincy Howe of the Columbia Broadcasting System has prepared a complete war chronology from Japan's invasion of Manchuria back in 1931 to the final surrender on the U.S.S. Missouri, and has written a running text to provide a factual background for pictures that tell their own story.*

March 1, 1946   Simon and Schuster, Inc.

INTRODUCTION

SINCE 1931, David Low has seen the world steadily and seen it whole. With an artistic skill matched only by his political insight, he has set down in black and white a running commentary and record of these "Years of Wrath." The first pages of this book show us the kind of world the war created: the world of 1946. The bulk of the book shows how we got that way.

"BABY PLAY WITH NICE BALL?"

This is the way the post-war world looks to David Low. The atomic bomb has become the symbol of our time and poses this simple question. Will mankind use the power of atomic energy for the purposes of total destruction or for the purposes of the more abundant life? Modern science has always posed this problem, but now it confronts us in a far more urgent form. The twentieth century has forced the human race to earn, all over again, the right to survive.

"WHY CAN'T WE WORK TOGETHER IN MUTUAL TRUST AND CONFIDENCE?"

On October 27, 1945, President Truman outlined a twelve-point American foreign policy. The passage that caused the widest interest dealt with the atomic bomb secret. Mr. Truman announced that the United States would regard the possession of that secret as a "sacred trust," but he did not propose sharing it with other nations. Prime Minister Attlee and Generalissimo Stalin did not care for the prospects but hoped for the best.

UNITED SURGERY IN GERMANY

Allied policy in Germany put Allied unity to its first practical postwar test. The Potsdam Declaration on Germany had called for treating the country as an economic unit. But Poland had acquired a large slice of eastern Germany and the French felt that the Ruhr and the Rhineland should be placed under international control. The Russians wanted a unified Germany; the British feared the consequences of a divided Germany. American policy vacillated.

BEHIND THE CURTAIN

When the foreign ministers of the Big Five powers met in London in September, 1945, Secretaries Byrnes and Bevin brought up the question of Russian policy in the former Axis satellites in Eastern Europe. Soviet Foreign Commissar Molotov insisted that the governments that the Russians had helped to establish in those countries enjoyed majority support, but his assurances did not convince the Anglo-Americans.

LOW'S NUREMBERG SKETCHBOOK—NO. 1

David Low visited the Nuremberg trials of the twenty-two Nazi big-shots accused of war crimes and made these drawings on the spot. The trials, conducted by legal experts from the four occupying powers, showed that the Allies could work together on two common purposes: punishment of the men chiefly responsible for promoting the Second World War and establishment of a whole new concept of "crimes against humanity."

STREICHER

FRANK

DÖNITZ

LOW'S NUREMBERG SKETCHBOOK—NO. 2

According to an article that David Low wrote from his ring-side seat at Nuremberg, Hermann Goering stood out as the strongest personality in the prisoners' dock. Former foreign minister Ribbentrop showed the most strain. Hess—who is shown here with folded arms—looked the craziest. The military and naval leaders appeared the most self-controlled. All the prisoners could wear earphones and listen to the proceedings in any one of four languages.

SON OF HEAVEN LEADS WORLD TO DEMOCRACY! FACE! BANZA!!

The first serious post-war job that the United States undertook was the occupation of Japan. Here, General MacArthur as Allied commander-in-chief wielded great power but he always acted under State Department directives. The other Allied powers also had representatives on the spot. The Allies used Emperor Hirohito to keep the Japanese people in line, but some people thought Hirohito himself should have been locked up as Japan's number one war criminal.

LOOKING TOWARDS WASHINGTON

When the Second World War ended only one major country escaped relatively unscathed—the United States of America. A stricken world therefore looked to Washington for immediate help in reconstruction and for longer-range planning and cooperation over the years. And from the point of view of the outside world, this drawing of David Low's does give a fair representation of American policy: question mark over the Capitol.

UNEASY STREET

T H E Second World War began on September 19, 1931, when Japanese troops marched into that part of northern China known as Manchuria. The trouble dated back to the Russian-Japanese War of 1905 when the Russians ceded to Japan special rights to various railroad lines and properties that they had previously acquired from the Chinese. One of these lines, the South Manchuria, had become the principal lever through which the Japanese exerted their power on China. Because the Japanese accused the Chinese of interference with their special rights on this railroad, Japanese troops marched against the Chinese and quickly seized key positions throughout Manchuria. Although Japan, America, and all the major European powers, except Russia, had agreed to respect Chinese independence and integrity, no immediate action followed this armed violation of Chinese rights. Indeed, the Chinese Government itself did not even break off relations with Japan.

THE "OPEN DOOR" POLICY IN CHINA

AT the turn of the century, Secretary of State John Hay of the United States wrote a series of notes to the major world powers of that time asking if they agreed with the American proposition that all of them should respect the territorial and administrative integrity of China and that all of them should trade with China on an equal basis. On receiving at least qualified acceptances from all the powers, Mr. Hay then published the entire correspondence and proclaimed the so-called "Open Door" policy in China which the United States has never formally renounced. But all the powers—including the United States —gave themselves considerable latitude in interpreting the Open Door and gradually whittled away Chinese independence. China's own civil wars assisted in this process until the nationalist resurgence of the 1920's culminated in the Chinese Revolution of 1926-27. The Japanese, thoroughly alarmed at the prospect of a unified, modern China therefore set themselves two tasks: to break up China and to expel all other foreign influence from the country. They believed in a one-way open door that let only themselves in and all other countries out.

THE RED CARPET

JAPAN's bid for world conquest, as this cartoon shows, hit the mass of the Chinese people more directly than it hit Britain and the United States. During the summer of 1931, Chinese officials made public the so-called "Tanaka Memorial," drawn up in 1928 by Prime Minister Tanaka of Japan, and outlining a detailed plan of world conquest. Here is one of its key passages, "The way to gain actual rights in Manchuria is to use this region as a base, and under the pretense of trade and commerce, penetrate the rest of China. Having China's entire resources at our disposal, we shall proceed to conquer India, the Archipelago, Asia Minor, Central Asia, and even Europe." General Honjo who commanded the Japanese invasion of Manchuria wrote to the Japanese war minister at that time, that Japan had to become economically self-sufficient by acquiring territories in Asia before declaring war on the United States.

HEAT WAVE

THE Japanese always took good care not to present their program of expansion purely in terms of their own national interests. They also tried to turn to their advantage the hostility that many Asiatics felt toward Europe and the United States. The Japanese therefore tried to monopolize for their own uses the slogan of "Asia for the Asiatics." To the Chinese the slogan meant an end of special privileges for the white nations which maintained their own courts on Chinese soil. To the Indians it meant independence from British rule. To the people of Malaya and the East Indies it meant freedom and a more abundant life. But the Europeans and Americans failed to come together in a common anti-Japanese front. Still more important, they felt such contempt for the Japanese that they did not recognize the latent appeal of the Asia for the Asiatics propaganda and thus made it easy for the Japanese to continue to undermine the prestige of the white race among millions of Asiatics who continued to regard themselves as the victims of imperial exploitation.

RULE JAPANNIA

IN January, 1932, Secretary of State Stimson tried to invoke the Nine-Power Treaty in connection with the Japanese invasion of Manchuria. Mr. Stimson declared that the Japanese had violated their agreement with the other major powers not to encroach upon the territorial or administrative integrity of China. The Japanese had undertaken this agreement at the Washington Naval Conference of 1922 which established a 5:5:3 ratio among the American, British, and Japanese Navies. The purpose of this agreement was to make each of these three powers impregnable in its own waters but unable to carry offensive naval warfare beyond its own sphere of influence. But Sir John Simon, the British Foreign Secretary, refused to follow Secretary Stimson's lead and declined to take common action with the United States against Japan's violation of the Nine-Power Treaty. This Anglo-American split then played into Japanese hands and permitted the Japanese, although the weakest of the three powers, to play one rival off against the other.

"PHEW! THAT'S A NASTY LEAK. THANK GOODNESS IT'S NOT AT OUR END OF THE BOAT."

ALTHOUGH the Wall Street crash of 1929 marked the official beginning of the World Depression, conditions in Middle Europe soon proved even more ominous. What had happened was this. The chief grain producing centers of Europe took nearly ten years to recover from the consequences of the First World War. Meanwhile, Argentina, Canada, and the United States had begun to increase their agricultural exports—and to reduce production costs by modern methods. The more backward farmers of Middle Europe could not meet this competition. The value of their land fell; so did the value of their mortgages. This at once affected the assets of the chief banking and credit institutions in Middle Europe. On top of this, the many small nations that had emerged from the First World War raised tariff walls and borrowed money to spend on armaments. A running sore thus began to develop in Middle Europe, but the West European powers and the United States did not recognize the danger to them—in time.

**"BETTER MAKE IT WIDE ENOUGH TO HOLD
YOURSELF TOO, BIG BOY."**

IN 1925, the League of Nations set up a preparatory commission to arrange
a disarmament conference and thus to promote one of the original aims of the
League—peace by disarmament. Seven years later, on February 2, 1932, that
conference met at Geneva. Sixty-three nations had been invited; thirty-one
attended. Hugh Gibson, head of the American delegation, proposed cutting all
land armies in two and outlawing tanks, chemicals, bombing planes, and heavy
artillery. Italy and Russia accepted the program. France and Britain rejected
it. Japan proposed that the British and Americans cut their Navies in two
and promised to reduce theirs to the same level—thus gaining naval equality
with the two major sea powers. The Conference adjourned in the middle of
July after voting, against German and Russian opposition, to condemn air and
gas warfare and to advocate naval reduction.

ENTER FATHER CHRISTMAS—MADE IN JAPAN

N O major power weathered the World Depression so successfully or so ruthlessly as Japan. Whereas the British and the Americans cut the values of their currencies 30% and 40%, the Japanese cut the gold content of the yen 60%. The living standards of Japanese workers declined still further, but they did have jobs and Japanese foreign trade enjoyed an unprecedented boom. For the first time in history, Britain no longer led the world in textile exports. European and American goods all but vanished from the markets of the Far East. Japanese exports to Latin America doubled and trebled. In Europe, rising tariff barriers could not exclude Japanese goods. Japan's drive for world trade started even before Japanese troops had marched into Manchuria. By the end of 1933, when this cartoon appeared, Japanese exports had hit an all-time high. Meanwhile world trade as a whole had declined to barely half the 1929 level.

THE ARYAN RACE—GERMANY 1933

ON March 5, 1933, the day after President Roosevelt's first inaugural, Hitler came to complete power in Germany after the Nazi and Nationalist Parties had won a majority of seats in the Reichstag elections. A month later, on April 1, the Nazi government declared its first one-day boycott of Jewish shops and businesses. But Hitler's racial doctrines had not yet spread, even in Germany, far beyond the ranks of the Nazi Party and he proceeded to develop them with the same combination of ruthlessness and caution that he applied in other fields. That is why Hitler is shown dragging old President von Hindenburg, while Franz von Papen, the Nationalist leader with whom the Nazis made the deal that brought them into power, clings to Hindenburg's neck. The fat figure out front is Ernst Röhm leader of the Brown Shirts who was shot in Hitler's presence on the bloody night of June 29-30, 1934.

COMPULSORY SPONTANEOUS DEMONSTRATION

ALTHOUGH both Hitler and Mussolini had the support of many conservatives who regarded their programs as a lesser evil than Communism, the Nazis and Fascists presented themselves as friends of the common man and staged great demonstrations on occasions like May Day. In the early stages of the Hitler regime, the Nazis therefore had to use threats and force to persuade the crowds to turn out and celebrate for them. This cartoon, which appeared in connection with Hitler's first May Day, not only reflects the way the outside world regarded the rise of Hitler at that time, it also gives a realistic picture of the condition of Germany itself. The Nazis were still arresting, imprisoning, and killing thousands of German Socialists and Communists in their concentration camps. They were gradually outlawing the Socialist and Communist Parties and all trade unions except their own. But the Nazis had to use force all the way down the line and they dealt with their opponents—at home and abroad—one at a time.

"NOW WOULD BE THE TIME TO CALL THE POLICE, KID—
HUH, HUH! IF THERE WERE ANY POLICE."

AS the year 1933 ran its course, all hope of disarmament went glimmering. Newspapers that had hopefully recorded the efforts of the Disarmament Conference turned their attention to one of the principal causes of its failure: the international traffic in arms. World statesmen had failed to get together. The armament makers in the different countries had no such difficulties. The French firm of Schneider-Creusot partially controlled the Czech firm of Skoda. Both concerns had shared their secrets with the German House of Krupp. Vickers and Imperial Chemicals dominated Britain—and Imperial Chemicals had a working agreement with the DuPont interests in the United States whereby the British concern sold to Europe, Asia, and Africa and the American concern sold only to the New World. In many other fields, international cartels fixed prices, divided markets, and restricted production. But in the armament field, these cartels sought to increase production by building up their competitors—and even buying into their competitor's businesses—and thus promoting suspicion and fear.

SIGNS OF RETURNING PROSPERITY

WHILE the industries of peace languished during the World Depression, war industries prospered. Economic distress and social disorder create distrust and fear of other nations. Anyone able to offer a man a job becomes a public benefactor in times of unemployment—and by October, 1933, when this cartoon appeared, the British armament industry had begun to expand and take up some of the unemployment slack in some of Britain's so-called "depressed areas." Of course, the arrival of Hitler in power gave Britain a legitimate reason to re-arm, but Hitler could never have come to power in Germany, or stayed there, without the support of German and foreign industrialists, many of whom worked together. There was a tendency when the revelations concerning the "Merchants of Death" first received wide attention to regard the "Secret International" of arms makers as an independent organization. But the arms makers were tied in with heavy industry generally, and the leaders of heavy industry did wield great power behind the scenes in Britain, France, and Germany throughout the 1930's.

THE CONFERENCE EXCUSES ITSELF

BY May, 1934, when this cartoon appeared, the Disarmament Conference had disintegrated. Japan had quit the League of Nations because it had refused to recognize the conquest of Manchuria. The Germans had resigned, too, because the League did not permit them to re-arm. The British National Government —nominally headed by Prime Minister MacDonald, actually controlled by Stanley Baldwin, leader of the Conservative Party, could not decide on any clear policy, but Foreign Secretary Simon usually propitiated the Germans and the Japanese. France had barely avoided civil war in February and a national coalition government headed by ex-President Doumergue had been voted wide powers. The Austrian government of Chancellor Dollfuss had crushed the powerful Socialist movement in Vienna. President Roosevelt gave his national recovery program for the United States priority over the world recovery program that European bankers had presented to the World Economic Conference of 1933—and had launched the biggest American program of naval construction since 1916.

THEY SALUTE WITH BOTH HANDS NOW

ON June 30, 1934, Hitler, Goering, and other leading Nazis executed a wide assortment of their opponents, inside the regime and out. Their victims included Captain Ernst Röhm who wanted to have his two million brown-shirted Storm Troopers assimilated by the German Army; former Chancellor von Schleicher and his wife who represented the more respectable elements in the German Army; Gregor Strasser, leader of the Nazi trade-union movement and advocate (along with the Brown Shirt leaders) of a "Second Revolution;" and Dr. Erich Klausener, head of the Catholic Action Society. On the one hand, Hitler wiped out the extremists within his own Party who wanted a more radical kind of revolution. On the other, he wiped out conservative oppositionists, especially in the Army and in Catholic circles. This cartoon, which appeared the day after the purge occurred, emphasizes the measures Hitler took against the Brown Shirts, but it presently became evident that the purge went much further than that.

HITLER: "The world still refuses to realise that violence, when used by Germans, is justified and righteous. What can I do? What would you do?"

EX-KAISER: "Do? I did."

THE PHILOSOPHY OF FORCE

TWENTY YEARS AFTER

THIS cartoon appeared on August 1, 1934, the twentieth anniversary of the German invasion of Belgium during the First World War. But even in a symbolic sense, a conversation between the Kaiser and Hitler is largely fantasy. One of the Kaiser's grandsons did join the Nazi Party. The Kaiser sent messages of congratulation to Hitler from time to time. But Hitler not only abused the Hohenzollerns in his speeches; his plans for conquest as outlined in *Mein Kampf* followed a different pattern than the Kaiser chose. Hitler berated the Kaiser for having gone to war with England, but unlike the Kaiser, he assumed that he would have to fight Russia. The Kaiser and his descendants never gave up hope of a Hohenzollern restoration. Hitler believed that the Third Reich he established would last a thousand years.

"See! Who will now deny that I have restored Germany to her former influence in European affairs!"

HITLERISM SHOWS RESULTS

DURING the summer of 1934 Foreign Minister Barthou of France made a tour of the capitals of Eastern Europe—including Moscow—that terminated in his assassination in the streets of Marseilles on October 9, side by side with King Alexander of Yugoslavia. Barthou's idea had been to create what he called an "Eastern Locarno" whereby the states of eastern Europe, backed by Britain, France, and the Soviet Union would agree to keep the peace, settle all differences by negotiation, and come to the aid of any victim of aggression. The British, however, blew cold on the scheme and the double assassination at Marseilles removed the two chief European advocates of that policy. By 1935, Pierre Laval who had become French Foreign Minister went to Moscow and without much enthusiasm signed a Franco-Soviet pact of mutual assistance for which Barthou had laid the groundwork. It marked the first counter-measure against Hitler's expansionist plans.

PROGRESS OF MAN, 1935 A.D.

THIS prophetic picture appeared on May 22, 1935. Mussolini had not yet launched his invasion of Ethiopia. He was merely piling up supplies with the knowledge and tacit consent of the British and French governments. Almost a year was to pass before German troops marched into the Rhineland and France lost its last chance to stop Hitler without war. The Nazis had not yet converted Germany from a peace to a war economy; they did not take that step until the remilitarization of the Rhineland convinced Hitler that the democracies would not fight. But German and Italian propagandists were stepping up their appeals to nationalism while the democracies, a little ashamed of nationalism themselves, did not dare or care to offer the people of the world a more humane and constructive program.

In Italy training in the arts of war now begins at the age of six; in Germany at ten.

FOSTER MOTHER

THE rising war spirit expressed itself in many ways during the 1930's, but above all it expressed itself in the extension of universal compulsory military service. This practise not only extended from country to country; the term of service was constantly being lengthened—with the Nazi and Fascist countries always in the lead. Democracies like Switzerland have always maintained conscription, but the Swiss have a citizen's army and do not inculcate their people with the war spirit from an early age. The Russians and French had maintained conscription for generations; they always depended for their security upon their armies. The British, on the other hand, used to rely on their fleet until Germany's preparations for air warfare caused them to double and triple their expenditures on the Royal Air Force in the mid-1930's. The British did not resort to conscription until 1938; The United States waited until 1940.

"ALL LI'! I AGREE! BUT ONLY UP TO HERE!"

BY the summer of 1935 when this cartoon appeared, the Japanese had occupied all of Manchuria, renamed it Manchukuo, and set up their own puppet government there. Their troops had also penetrated Jehol Province, to the south, and were taking over all of China north of the Great Wall. The Chinese National Government, with its capital at Nanking, still maintained formal relations with Japan and Generalissimo Chiang Kai-shek was devoting more energy to fighting Chinese Communists than to opposing the Japanese. But there was little that the Chinese could do to stop the Japanese, because the foreign powers, with interests in China, declined to bring even economic pressure to bear against Japan. The Chinese therefore played for time and made what arrangements they could with the Japanese.

JAPANESE aggression always rested on a base of human exploitation to which few Americans or Europeans would long submit. Hitler slaughtered the opposition leaders in Germany. Mussolini jailed most anti-Fascists and murdered others. But Hitler and Mussolini both offered some hope to the German and Italian people and even cut down unemployment and improved the condition of some of their people. Japan's militarists, on the other hand, did not even pretend to benefit the lot of the common man in Japan. Industrial workers lived like slaves in barracks. Peasants barely kept body and soul together tilling the soil. Japan also required many more imports than Germany—and had to feed a larger population on half as much arable land. No wonder Japan's economic system looked shaky. The miracle was that it held up so long and carried such a heavy load.

"LET US EXTEND OUR HAND TO GERMANY"

BY 1935, the British National Government, in which the Conservative Party was playing an ever-increasing role, was showing more and more tendency to do business with Hitler. This government signed a Naval Agreement with Germany, violating the Versailles Treaty and a much more recent Anglo-French Treaty whereby Britain and France pledged themselves to consult each other in matters affecting their policy toward Europe. The British, however, recognized the right of Germany to build a fleet 35% as large as their own and did not inform the French in advance. Shortly afterward a delegation of British ex-service men visited Germany and in certain circles the words "Let us extend our hand to Germany" became a kind of slogan. Many British Liberals and Laborites believed that their country had not given the German Republic a break. Now the Conservatives were giving Hitler a better deal than the Weimar Republic ever got.

THE KEY

THIS cartoon appeared on September 2, 1935. A week later, Sir Samuel Hoare, the British Foreign Secretary, pledged his country to "steady and collective resistance to agression." Early in October Mussolini sent Italian armies into Ethiopia. At this point, everyone connected with the League of Nations and even a good many people who had never expressed much confidence in any kind of "internationalism" joined in demanding the imposition of economic sanctions against Italy. The Covenant of the League of Nations does not specifically authorize the use of force against any aggressor. The whole idea of the League was that economic sanctions, universally applied, could prevent war. But the ultra-conservatives of every country—and not of England only—insisted that sanctions would lead to war and their view finally prevailed.

THE MAN. WHO TOOK THE LID OFF

THE Second World War began in Asia when the Japanese invaded Manchuria on September 19, 1931. It spread to Africa when the Italians invaded Ethiopia on October 1, 1935. And the consequences of Mussolini's decision to invade Ethiopia at once had repercussions in Europe. Although all members of the League of Nations did not apply economic sanctions, Italy's position quickly deteriorated. Mussolini had to turn to Hitler for help and placed himself under obligations that led within a year to the development of the so-called Rome-Berlin Axis.

SUEZCIDE?

ONE key to Mussolini's policy and character lay in his conviction that he could restore to Italy its ancient lordship over the Mediterranean. But his conquest of Ethiopia not only led him further afield than any Caesar had ever ventured; in attacking Ethiopia, Mussolini was also challenging a British vital interest. At the moment, the British did not meet that challenge. They even permitted Italian vessels to carry troops and supplies for the Ethiopian campaign through the Suez Canal. But the British did not forget the humiliation that they suffered at Mussolini's hands or his demand for a share in the administration of Suez.

THE GIRLS HE LEFT BEHIND HIM

NOBODY welcomed Mussolini's decision to invade Ethiopia more warmly than Hitler. Not only did it mean that the Italians finally had to mortgage themselves to the Germans, it meant that Mussolini had left the gate into Central Europe wide open to Hitler. This marked a complete reversal of Italian policy. In July, 1934, Austrian Nazis, acting under German instructions, assassinated Chancellor Dollfuss of Austria and tried to take over. Mussolini at once mobilized the Italian armies on Austria's frontier and Hitler drew back. Immediately afterward, Hitler and Mussolini held their first meeting—on Italian, not on German soil. Both of them pledged themselves to respect Austrian independence, and it was Mussolini's Ethiopian gamble that gave Hitler his chance to break that pledge.

"THE STRENGTH OF A CHAIN IS THAT OF ITS WEAKEST LINK."

NO sooner had the League of Nations begun to impose economic sanctions against Italy in October, 1935, than the ranks began to break. Pierre Laval, the French Foreign Minister, had negotiated an agreement with Italy a few months before. He attached much more importance to this than he did to the agreement with Russia that he inherited from his predecessor, Louis Barthou. And by the end of 1935, Pierre Laval and Sir Samuel Hoare, the British Foreign Secretary, were to produce their short-lived agreement to turn over three-quarters of Ethiopia to Mussolini. Anthony Eden, to whom Laval is clinging with one hand in this picture, occupied the special Cabinet post of Minister of League of Nations Affairs. He, like Russian Foreign Commissar Litvinov who is shown clinging to Laval's legs was, at this period, among the most vigorous champions of collective security.

PACIFISM IS NOT ENOUGH

THE policy of strong League sanctions against Italy met with two different kinds of opposition in Great Britain. Sir Samuel Hoare, Lord Vansittart, and other Conservatives hoped to bring Mussolini into closer relations with themselves and the French. If there had to be war, they preferred to have Germany fight Russia, and with that end in view they first propitiated Mussolini and then Hitler. They also feared that any war would ultimately prove fatal to British interests, and they believed sanctions against Italy ran that risk. Then a large number of British pacifists advocated peace at any price, and opposed taking any action at all—even an economic boycott against Italy. An organization of non-resisters known as the Peace Pledge Union made considerable progress after the Ethiopian affair and received a lot of publicity. But it never commanded anything like the support of the League of Nations Union which secured 11 million signatures during the spring of 1935 to a resolution calling for peace through collective security.

S.O.S.

IN November, 1935, the British held their first general election since 1931, when a split in the Labor Party set the stage for the National Government, formally headed by Ramsay MacDonald but actually controlled by the Conservatives. By 1935, the Labor Party had recovered somewhat from the rout it suffered in the 1931 voting, but the Conservatives won more than twice as many seats as Labor held in the House of Commons. The Conservatives owed part of their success to their endorsement of the principle of collective security which Anthony Eden, as Minister for League of Nations Affairs, promoted rather more vigorously than Sir Samuel Hoare, the Foreign Secretary. These are the two figures looking out to sea on the raft. The other two are Low's famous character, Colonel Blimp, and Lord Beaverbrook, proprietor of the Daily Express and advocate of Empire Free Trade, isolation from Europe, a free hand for Germany and Italy, and non-cooperation with the Soviet Union.

"YOU KNOW YOU CAN TRUST ME."

IN November, 1935, the Conservative Party won a huge majority of seats in the House of Commons. It had pledged itself, among other things, to a policy of "steady and collective resistance to aggression" and had the support of many genuine League of Nations' enthusiasts—notably Lord Robert Cecil. Less than a month after the election, however, news leaked into the press that Foreign Secretary Sir Samuel Hoare had entered into an agreement with Premier Laval of France to turn most of Ethiopia over to Italy, although the League of Nations had already named Italy the aggressor. Hoare had to resign at once and the whole Conservative Government, headed by Stanley Baldwin, nearly fell. Baldwin had taken over the coalition National Government from Ramsay MacDonald and the words "Trust Baldwin" had become the chief Conservative slogan. Mr. Baldwin disclaimed personal responsibility for the Hoare-Laval deal and admitted it had been a mistake.

"GUNS OR BUTTER?"

AS a matter of fact, it was Goering, not Hitler, who first declared that if Germany had to choose between guns or butter, guns would be the choice. But it was Hitler who ousted Dr. Schacht as Minister of Economics in 1936 and replaced him with Goering. Schacht had served his purpose by promoting German foreign trade and putting through a public works program that provided Germany with the industrial plant required for war production. When Goering came into the picture, Schacht had laid the economic foundations of a war economy and Goering's main job was to build that economy up to all-out, total war production.

STEPPING STONES TO GLORY

BY the summer of 1936, when this cartoon appeared, Hitler had taken the step that assured Germany's western frontier against attack from France. German troops had re-occupied the Rhineland in early March, and German engineers were building up its fortifications. Hitler ordered this move into the Rhineland against the advice of all his military commanders who had instructions to pull their troops out at once if the French made any hostile move. But France had been undergoing a series of Cabinet crises and Hitler ordered the move into the Rhineland at a moment when the French were making one of their periodic changes of government. And the British had not encouraged the French to take a strong stand.

THE PATRIOTS

THE Spanish Civil War began with an army revolt on July 19, 1936. General Francisco Franco, commander of the army in the Spanish zone of Morocco, landed at Cadiz with Foreign Legion and Moorish troops and called for an uprising against the Popular Front government—a coalition of Socialists, Communists, Syndicalists, liberals, and republicans—which had won a majority of seats in the elections to the Cortes that spring. Many garrisons and part of the navy joined the rebels who soon captured the western half of the country. But General Franco always lacked native Spanish manpower and when his original followers failed to overthrow the Republic within a few weeks as they had anticipated, the Italians and the Germans who had been equipping him from the start moved in.

"EXCELLENCY, THE MOORISH TROOPS ARE DISTURBED — THEY SAY OUR CONDUCT OF THE WAR IS UNCHRISTIAN....."

PROGRESS OF "CIVILIZATION" IN SPAIN

T H E month of November, 1936, when this cartoon appeared, witnessed one of the most critical struggles in the Spanish Civil War—the battle of Madrid. Early that month, Germany and Italy both recognized the Franco government and with their airplanes a series of civilian bombings began that brought widespread revulsion and condemnation. During the height of the battle for Madrid—which the Loyalists continued to hold—President Roosevelt, Secretary Hull, and Undersecretary Phillips framed the Embargo Act, which prevented the Loyalists from purchasing any war supplies from the United States. On the one hand, the United States government did not regard the war in Spain as an international affair and therefore did not apply sanctions to Italy or Germany. On the other hand, it did not regard it as a civil war and therefore did not sell arms to the Spanish Republic. The Neutrality Act did not apply. A special act had to be put through Congress to cover this special situation.

THE NON-INTERVENTION COMMITTEE DECIDE TO WAIT UNTIL THE WAR ENDS BEFORE TAKING A FIRM STAND.

OLD LOW'S ALMANACK: PROPHECIES FOR 1937

THE British and French governments found another formula for giving indirect aid to Franco in the Spanish Civil War. The British took the lead in setting up a Non-Intervention Committee, ostensibly designed to localize the fighting by attempting to prevent arms shipments to either side. The Germans and Italians at once joined the Non-Intervention Committee and continued to pour war supplies and soldiers into Rebel Spain. The British shipped nothing. The Russians exchanged some war supplies for some Spanish gold and sent in some military advisors to the Loyalists. The Communist Parties all over the world also sent men and supplies to the Loyalists. The French occasionally opened their frontier to shipments from Russia and Czechoslovakia. And while the munition trade boomed and tens of thousands of foreign troops poured into Spain, the Non-Intervention Committee continued its deliberations under the chairmanship of Lord Plymouth in London.

SEEING RED

A MONTH after the Spanish Civil War broke out, the more reactionary British papers (and the more reactionary papers in other countries, too) were representing every sympathizer with the Spanish Loyalist cause as a Communist. Even Prime Minister Baldwin, who is shown scratching the back of his head, and Foreign Secretary Eden were suspects. And Léon Blum, the new Socialist Premier of France who is shown holding the little flag labelled "Democracy," was regarded with great suspicion. But as time passed, the British government was destined to look at Spain through the same tinted glasses that the Reader of the *Daily Scarlet Fever* uses. All of which played into the hands of the extremists in Spain and everywhere else.

COOKED TOUR

AS the year 1936 drew to a close, Stanley Baldwin's irresolute foreign policy was causing more and more alarm. By the middle of November when this cartoon appeared, the British government had decided to ship no war materials to the Spanish Loyalists, and Hitler's remilitarization of the Rhineland was well under way. Harold Laski, leading brain truster of the Labor Party, told a revealing Baldwin story at this time. He said that when someone had pointed out to Mr. Baldwin some of the dangers to which his policy was exposing his country, Mr. Baldwin replied, "That is a problem for my successor."

"HOW MUCH WILL YOU GIVE ME NOT TO KICK YOUR PANTS FOR, SAY, TWENTY-FIVE YEARS?"

AFTER Germany had remilitarized the Rhineland, Hitler gained an initiative in European affairs that none of his predecessors under the Weimar Republic had enjoyed. While planning and preparing for new moves and finally for war, Hitler would occasionally try to represent himself as a man of peace by suggesting a twenty-five year non-aggression pact in exchange for colonies, loans, and spheres of influence in Europe. But his long record of broken promises prevented this plan from getting anywhere. In all likelihood, he did not expect to gain anything abroad but he hoped that these professions of peace would gain support among his own people.

BUSINESS RECESSION

ON November 25, 1936, Germany, Italy, and Japan signed their three-power anti-Comintern Pact to which Hungary and Spain later adhered. The pact grew out of Germany's withdrawal from the League of Nations and subsequent support of Italy during the Ethiopian war. Japan had quit the League over the Manchurian affair; Italy over the affair in Ethiopia. The three countries then entered into a loose kind of political and military alliance that led to more or less close collaboration among their foreign offices and military establishments. But no other major powers joined the group, and its appeals for direct financial help from Britain and the United States got nowhere. The anti-Russian, anti-Communist line that the Axis powers followed attracted some sympathy abroad for political reasons. But the economic weaknesses of the German-Italian-Japanese combination blocked much material aid.

THE AUTOGRAPH COLLECTOR

BY January, 1937, a year after he had replaced Sir Samuel Hoare as Foreign Secretary, Anthony Eden had substantially adopted Prime Minister Baldwin's policy of conciliation which developed over the years into Neville Chamberlain's policy of appeasement. Eden visited many foreign capitals; wrote messages to many foreign statesmen, asking them to sign agreements not worth the paper on which they were written.

THIS cartoon appeared on February 2, 1937, three months after the Spanish Loyalists had successfully beaten off a Rebel offensive against Madrid and at the time they routed Italian troops at Guadalajara. By and large, however, the Loyalists had fought a losing defensive battle during the first six months of the Civil War. What these losses meant to the British Empire did not become fully apparent until several more years had passed. But David Low was not the only person to recognize, even back in 1937, that the establishment of a hostile power in Spain would threaten the British Empire's Mediterranean life-line.

"WE MUST KEEP A COOL HEAD TO THE UTMOST"—
says The PRIME MINISTER

THE QUESTION OF TEMPERATURE

IN June, 1937 Prime Minister Baldwin turned over his Conservative Government to his Chancellor of the Exchequer, Neville Chamberlain. Anthony Eden remained Foreign Secretary and both he and his new chief had little choice but to continue the policies to which Mr. Baldwin had already deeply committed his country and his party. Neville Chamberlain's elder half-brother, Sir Austen Chamberlain, had served as Foreign Secretary under Baldwin in the 1920's and had always shown a strong partiality for France and Anthony Eden got his start in politics as Sir Austen's secretary. The Chamberlain family did not belong to the landed aristocracy from which most British political leaders had come. They made their fortune in the manufacturing industries of Birmingham. It was this commercial background that accounted in part for Neville Chamberlain's conciliatory attitude toward Hitler and Mussolini whom he dealt with as commercial rivals rather than as national enemies.

REVIVAL OF OLD-TIME MELODRAMA

WITHIN a year after the non-intervention agreement on Spain went into effect, Italian submarines were sinking British merchant vessels that tried to run the blockade into Loyalist Spain. The British vessels making the run to Spain were proceeding at their own risk, but the Italians had no authority under the non-intervention agreement to send their navy into action against the merchant ships of a friendly power. The British and Russians who had both lost vessels to Italian submarines therefore forced the non-intervention committee to meet at the French city of Nyon and stop the sinkings. Had such a measure been invoked earlier and maintained more scrupulously, the war in Spain might have turned out differently. But the British attitude at Nyon was the exception; the condition depicted above was the rule.

"DO YOU SMELL SOMETHING BURNING?"

THE agreement that Chiang Kai-shek worked out with the Chinese Communists at the end of 1936 paid substantial dividends when the Japanese opened their big offensive against central China seven months later. For the Communists applied against the Japanese the same guerrilla tactics they had already perfected in fighting Chiang. These tactics consisted of always avoiding a direct engagement with enemy troops but always attacking enemy communications or outposts. Chiang's own German advisors recommended just such tactics. The result was that the Japanese never extended their control over the parts of China they occupied beyond the confines of the larger cities and the immediate vicinity of the principal communication lines. This of course disrupted Chinese life, but it prevented the Japanese from gaining much benefit from their occupation.

IN July, 1937, the Japanese dropped all pretense that their ambitions in Asia did not go beyond Manchuria or northern China. Their troops marched across the so-called Marco Polo Bridge at Peiping.and opened a general campaign against the National Government of Chiang Kai-shek. This government had greatly strengthened itself as the result of the kidnapping of Chiang Kai-shek by the "Young Marshal," Chang Hsueh-Liang—son of the Manchurian war lord Chang Tso-lin whom the Japanese had murdered back in 1929. The Young Marshal persuaded Chiang to call off his anti-Communist campaigns and make a common front with the Communists against the Japanese. The Japanese, seeing China well on the way toward national unity, therefore embarked on their all-out war against China. And the Japanese had achieved national unity of a sort. A group of young army officers failed in their attempted coup d'etat at the end of February, 1936, shortly after the moderate parties had made a good showing in the elections. But the more experienced militarists moved in and Imperial Japan held no more elections.

STANDING ROOM ONLY

DURING the First World War, the British Government issued the famous "Balfour Declaration" promising to support the development of a Jewish National Home in Palestine. At the same time, Colonel T. E. Lawrence had committed the British to support the cause of Arab independence. There is no conflict or contradiction between these two commitments, but at the Peace Conference the Arabs felt the British had let them down. The British could ill afford to offend either group, but Arab good-will appeared more important to Britain's imperial interests—partly because British rule in India rests to some extent on the good-will of the Moslem minority, partly because British control of the Mediterranean and the Middle East requires the support of the Arabs in that part of the world. Successive British Governments therefore tended to restrict the rights of the Jews in Palestine and to give the Arabs a better break. In July, 1937, when this cartoon appeared, Colonial Secretary Ormsby-Gore was preparing the way for the settlement that the British finally proposed in March, 1939, whereby the Jews would become a national minority in an Arab state.

NEW LIGHT ON EVOLUTION

T H E story of the years between 1919 and 1939 might well be entitled *The Decline and Fall of the League of Nations*. When President Wilson came to Paris in 1918 with his Fourteen Points and his proposed League of Nations, the war-weary peoples believed he was ushering in a new world. The Versailles Treaty which finally emerged in June, 1919, fell measurably short of expectations. But the admission of Germany to the League of Nations and Foreign Minister Stresemann's policy of conciliation with Germany's former enemies led to a revival of hope during the 1920's. In the 1930's, however, these hopes dwindled and pretty well vanished when Italy invaded Ethiopia in the face of League opposition. This cartoon expressed the gloom that had settled on many Englishmen by September, 1937, when it first appeared.

BLASPHEMY! NOT FIT FOR YOUNG EARS!

SPEAKING at Chicago on October 5, 1937, President Roosevelt called for a "quarantine" of "aggressor nations" and announced that the United States was prepared to take an active part in the search for peace. His address received wider support in democratic countries than it did in the United States. Winston Churchill said it expressed "in eloquent language exactly the same idea that is in our minds." Germany, Italy, and Japan on the other hand played the speech down, except in so far as they used it to intensify their attacks on all aggressive exponents of democracy who became, from then on, "war-mongers." It was by shutting off the truth from the younger generation and by filling young people with their own war-like ideas that the Germans and Japanese in particular were able to develop such fanatical young soldiers.

Great Britain and every country owe a
debt of gratitude...for the encouragement
given to sport by this exhibition.
— LORD HALIFAX

NAZI HUNTING EXHIBITION

IN 1937, Lord Halifax embarked on one of the most pathetic missions ever undertaken by the statesman of a major power. As Lord Privy Seal in the Chamberlain Government, he went to Germany to attend a hunting expedition sponsored by Goering. He also took the opportunity to drop in on Hitler, too. In spite of the dubious impressions that Halifax brought back from Germany, Prime Minister Chamberlain felt he had no choice but to continue his policy of appeasement. Goering's hunting exploits did occasion one flash of wit by the British Ambassador in Berlin—Sir Neville Henderson. One day Goering told Henderson he had just enjoyed some fine shooting. "Animals, I presume?" Henderson replied.

FOREIGN POLICY VAUDEVILLE ACT

D U R I N G the fall of 1937 while Foreign Secretary Eden was attending a Far
Eastern Conference at Brussels that failed to halt Japanese aggression in Asia,
Prime Minister Chamberlain sent Lord Halifax, Lord Privy Seal in his Cabinet,
on a series of missions to appease the Rome-Berlin Axis. Lord Halifax, formerly
Sir Robert Irwin, had gained fame as the first viceroy of India willing to sit
down with Gandhi and reach an agreement. A High Church Anglican of deep
religious conviction, and at the same time a Tory of the Tories, Lord Halifax
enjoyed the confidence of many different groups. Here he is shown helping
Mr. Chamberlain balance two factions in the Conservative Party. On the left
we have the so-called "Cliveden Set" of which the London *Times,* under the
editorship of Sir Geoffrey Dawson was the chief mouthpiece. On the right are
the ultra-imperialists who paid as little attention as possible to Europe and
thought chiefly in terms of Empire First.

MASS MURDER IN CHINA

THE large-scale campaign that the Japanese launched in China in the summer of 1937 hit Anglo-American interests as well as the interests of the Chinese. A Japanese airplane machine-gunned the automobile carrying the British Ambassador to China, who barely survived his wounds. In December, more Japanese planes sunk the American gunboat *Panay* as it was escorting a group of Standard Oil tankers up the Yangtse River. Throughout this period, the British and American governments talked of "parallel action" but it consisted mainly of selling war supplies to both groups of belligerents—with the Japanese proving the better customers. This did not bring the American Neutrality Act into operation because even during all this savage warfare, the Chinese and Japanese governments had not formally declared war on each other.

NEMESIS RESTAURANT

BY January, 1938, when this cartoon appeared, Japan had completed the conquest of Manchuria and had moved on into central China. Italy had also proclaimed Ethiopia part of the new Fascist Empire. In short, Japan had upset the balance of power in Asia. Italy had upset the balance of power in the Mediterranean. The civil war in Spain was moving inexorably against the Loyalists and Hitler did not wait long to cash in on a situation that increasingly favored the aggressor.

INCREASING PRESSURE

THIS cartoon appeared on February 18, 1938, two days before Foreign Secretary Eden resigned his post to protest the failure of the Chamberlain Government to come to the aid of Austria. On February 12, Chancellor Schuschnigg—who is made to represent his country in this picture—had conferred with Hitler at Berchtesgaden where he agreed to admit the Austrian Nazi, Arthur Seyss-Inquart to his Cabinet as Minister of the Interior and Public Safety. The long-nosed figure representing France is Foreign Minister Bonnet who tried to accommodate Hitler to the bitter end.

"THOUGH EVERY PROSPECT PLEASES"(?)

I T was not at the hands of his enemies but at the hands of his partner in the Rome-Berlin Axis that Mussolini received the first serious set-backs of his diplomatic career. Mussolini had backed Austrian independence under both the Dollfuss and the Schuschnigg governments. But his Ethiopian adventure and his break with the League of Nations forced him into dependence on Hitler and by the end of February, 1938, when this cartoon appeared, Mussolini had no choice but to accept the absorption of Austria by Germany. This meant that Italy and Germany had a common frontier at the Brenner Pass which later became a favorite meeting-spot for the two dictators.

The Government must go ahead on the course which they have chosen..... I wish them success."— *EDEN*.

"ME TOO"

T H E resignation of Anthony Eden as British Foreign Secretary on February 20, 1938 might have overthrown the Chamberlain Government, if Mr. Eden had made an issue of Chamberlain's consent to Germany's absorption of Austria. Eden's refusal to demand a vote of confidence led some people to accuse him of "hanging himself with his old school tie." Others, however, doubted that Eden had the nation—much less a majority in a predominantly Conservative House of Commons—behind him. It is important to remember that Eden took office when public clamor over the Hoare-Laval Pact forced Sir Samuel Hoare from the Foreign Office and that he continued the Conservative Party's policy of conciliation toward Germany. Not until Neville Chamberlain insisted on continuing this policy when Hitler threatened the independence of Austria did Eden feel that it was time for a change.

THE POLICY THAT DIDN'T COME OFF

WHEN Hitler invaded Austria on March 11, 1938, Lord Halifax who succeeded Anthony Eden as Foreign Secretary was reported to have paced the Foreign Office with his head in his hands saying, "Horrible, horrible, I never thought they'd do it." With Mr. Eden in opposition to the Chamberlain policy of appeasement was Winston Churchill who had been warning Britain against German re-armament ever since Hitler took power. Mr. Churchill described Mr. Chamberlain at this time as "a good Lord Mayor of Birmingham in a lean year."

NOT ONLY THE AUSTRIANS VOTED

WHEN Chancellor Schuschnigg threatened to hold an Austrian plebiscite early in March, 1938 to determine whether or not the people supported his government, Hitler at once took the country over. A month later he staged a plebiscite of his own. Meanwhile, Mussolini, Chamberlain, Halifax, and Daladier were accepting the fate of Austria in much the same spirit as the Austrian people themselves. This was particularly true of Mussolini who lost what little freedom of action he enjoyed, in relation to Germany, the moment Hitler established a common frontier on the Brenner Pass.

"SORRY, BUT WE DON'T WANT TO BURN OUR FINGERS."

ON March 17, 1938, the Soviet Union proposed an immediate international conference, minus Germany, Italy, and Japan, to discuss the menace of aggression to world peace. The Chamberlain Government, however, cold-shouldered this proposal as it had cold-shouldered similar offers of Russian co-operation. The supporters of this refusal justified it with the argument that the purges of many Russian political and military leaders had made the Soviet Union an undependable factor in world affairs. Critics of Chamberlain argued that the Conservatives feared and hated Communism more than they feared and hated Fascism.

"...HE TOOK WATER AND WASHED HIS HANDS...."

THIS cartoon appeared four days after Britain and Italy signed a pact of peace and harmony at Rome on April 20, 1938. The British promised to work through the League of Nations for recognition of the Italian conquest of Ethiopia. Italy agreed to withdraw all armed forces and war materials from Spain on the conclusion of the civil war. This marked an attempt on the part of the British to return to the policy of the Hoare-Laval Pact. The British not only wanted Italian co-operation in the Mediterranean, they still hoped they might pry Mussolini loose from the Axis and then force Hitler to come to terms, too. But these plans excluded Russia and would therefore have led, ultimately, to a Russo-German war, with the western democracies and the Italians backing the Germans.

"YOU'VE GOT TO ADMIT I'M BRINGING PEACE TO THE POOR SUFFERING BASQUES."

N O episode in the Spanish civil war aroused more indignation abroad than the destruction of the Basque city of Guernica by German planes. Guernica possessed no military importance. It had no defenses against air attack. But it gave the German air force an opportunity to demonstrate the effectiveness of air bombardment. And the crowning irony was this. The supporters of General Franco represented him as the defender of Christianity, yet the Germans chose as their target of attack the most devoutly Catholic region in all of Spain. It was also in the Basque country that St. Ignatius Loyola was born.

"WOULD YOU OBLIGE ME WITH A MATCH, PLEASE?"

THIS eloquent cartoon tells its own story. And it is no libel on democracy in the later 1930's to identify it with the person of Neville Chamberlain who became the symbol of a policy for which he did not bear sole responsibility. Mr. Chamberlain not only inherited an accumulation of Prime Minister Baldwin's errors. He knew—as his wistful attitude toward the photograph of Anthony Eden suggests—that he was heading into trouble. Finally, British public opinion was itself as divided and uncertain as the policy that both Mr. Baldwin and Mr. Chamberlain followed.

"SHUT UP! I CAN'T HEAR MYSELF!"

PROPAGANDA Minister Goebbels made so much noise about his own propaganda that it received wide attention in the world press. At the same time, many democratic spokesmen complained that their propaganda could not be heard above the din. Propaganda in those days had a bad name: a hangover from some of the false stories that all belligerents put out during the First World War. In the course of time, however, the Goebbels propaganda tended to defeat itself whereas the democracies suffered less from faulty propaganda technique than from lack of a clear program.

THE key to this cartoon lies under Adolf Hitler's chair. When Hitler, Chamberlain, Daladier, and Mussolini met at Munich to partition Czechoslovakia for the benefit of Germany, they had a larger purpose in view. It was to create a four-power pact to replace the League of Nations or any other system of collective security and to leave the Soviet Union out in the cold. Most liberals and radicals in both France and England opposed the Munich settlement because they saw in this exclusion of Russia an invitation to Germany to strike east. Most conservatives in both countries supported Munich, partly because they thought it had prevented war; partly because they thought that if it finally came to war, Germany and Russia would be the principle antagonists and that their countries could keep out.

AFTER MUNICH

THIS cartoon appeared on October 3, 1938, two days before Edouard Benes
resigned as President of Czechoslovakia. Seven months before, Chancellor
Schuschnigg of Austria had been ousted by the same forces that caused the
downfall of Czechoslovakia, and two years before Germany destroyed Austrian
independence, Emperor Haile Selassie had fled from Ethiopia before Mussolini's armies. In a farewell broadcast to the people of Czechoslovakia, Dr.
Benes said, "I have no intention of analysing the whole political situation
which has led me to this decision. I shall just say in short that the whole system
of balance of power in Europe, established after the war, has steadily weakened for several years. In the last three years it has basically changed to the
disadvantage of ourselves and our friends."

I will be good

(SIGNED)

Adolf Hitler

BRITAIN'S NEW DEFENSE

THIS cartoon appeared less than a week after the Munich Conference knocked down the breach in Czechoslovakia through which Hitler moved in to dominate Central Europe and cut connections between the Soviet Union and the Western powers. The man shown leaping over the rope held by Neville Chamberlain and Lord Halifax is Sir John Simon, who turned down Secretary Stimson's proposals for joint action against Japan in 1932 and who became one of the most consistent advocates of appeasement under the successive governments of MacDonald, Baldwin, and Chamberlain. A former member of the Liberal Party, Sir John joined forces with the Conservatives when the pound went off the gold standard in September, 1931. As he crossed the floor from the opposition benches to the government side of the House of Commons, Lloyd George declared that he was the only man in his memory who, as he crossed the floor, "left a trail of slime behind him." On another occasion Lloyd George also remarked that Sir John "has sat so long upon the fence that the iron has entered into his soul."

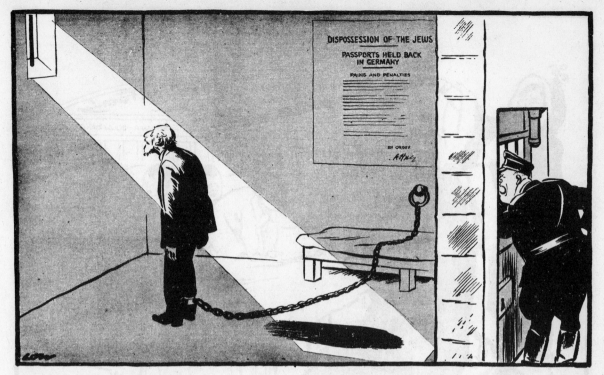

"WHY DON'T YOU GO?"

DURING the month of November, 1938, a month after the Munich Conference, the Nazis staged one of their most savage offensives against the Jews. Seizing upon the assassination in Paris of a German consular official, Vom Rath, by Herschel Grynszpan, a half-crazed Polish Jew of seventeen, the Nazis confiscated virtually all the private property owned by Jews in Germany. The assassination occurred on November 7; by November 10 almost every Jewish synagogue and business establishment in Germany had been wrecked. The government then proceeded to fine the Jews of Germany one billion marks, or about $400,000,000 for the destruction of their own property. At the same time, the Nazis continued to blame the Jews for undermining the National Socialist state while at the same time they refused to let any Jew leave the country with any property. This led to the withdrawal of the American Ambassador from Berlin and caused a popular revulsion in Great Britain against the Chamberlain appeasement policy.

"EUROPE CAN LOOK FORWARD TO A CHRISTMAS OF PEACE."
—(HITLER)

AFTER the Munich Conference, Hitler promised Europe a Christmas of peace. But it was a peace bought at the expense of Britain and France. The words "Ex French-British Family" refer to the Versailles system of alliances that Hitler destroyed. The Little Entente of Czechoslovakia, Rumania, and Yugoslavia looked mainly to France for support. So did Poland. Allied loans had several times saved Austria and Hungary. Britain maintained especially close relations with Greece and Turkey. Bulgaria looked to the Little Entente and to Russia. But Germany's absorption of Austria and the partition of Czechoslovakia had knocked the props out from under this whole system.

THE MAN WHO HEARS VOICES

THIS representation of Hitler as one who hears voices rests on solid fact. The voices, however, came from within. He long believed that occult forces ruled the world and based his own career on the advice of astrologers and fortune-tellers. The Nazi emblem, for instance, is a reversed swastika which—unlike the true swastika—does not represent the principle of fertility but the principle of destruction. While Hitler was still an obscure organizer in the early 1920's he constantly turned for advice to a Jewish astrologer who had changed his name from Steinschneider to Hanussen and who met a violent end. Marshal Goering gave Hitler the highest praise he knew of when he said the Fuehrer proceeded with *"nachtwandlerischer Sicherheit"*—the security of the sleep-walker.

"HIMMEL! IS THAT ME?"

THE Nazis owed much of their power in Germany to the fact that they identified all Germans with the Nazi ideal. During the 1930's some of the better elements in Germany were able either to escape into exile or go into opposition inside Germany. But the exiles lost touch with Germany; the opposition got nowhere. When war came, most of the German people thus found themselves committed to Hitler's policies.

AURORA AMERICANSIS

AT the beginning of 1938, the appropriations for the United States Navy totalled more than half a billion dollars: ever since his first months in the White House, President Roosevelt had always given a high priority to building up American naval strength. And in January, 1939, Congress followed the President's lead and voted to spend a round billion dollars on naval expansion. Experts already calculated that the United States would need to treble these expenditures to carry a successful singlehanded offensive into Japanese waters. That was one time that history proved the experts were right.

BY the end of 1938 when this cartoon appeared, Prime Minister Chamberlain began to hope that his appeasement policy really had brought "Peace in Our Time." Premier Daladier of France, on the other hand, took a more skeptical view as Italian students and deputies were shouting for Tunisia, Corsica, and Nice. But Mussolini had staged these demonstrations for their nuisance value only. When he presented his own demands he asked for more favorable adjustments in Tunis, the Suez Canal, and Jibuti.

GOOD OLD ITALIAN HOSPITALITY

IN the middle of January, 1939, Prime Minister Chamberlain and Foreign Secretary Halifax visited Mussolini in Rome. At the time of Munich, Mussolini had served as the intermediary between Hitler on the one hand and Chamberlain and Daladier on the other. Chamberlain therefore hoped that he might pry Mussolini loose from Hitler or at least bring Italy closer to Britain and France. But the opponents of appeasement feared that Chamberlain would simply make more concessions and get nothing in return.

"HONEST, MISTER, THERE'S NOBODY HERE BUT
US SPANIARDS."

HAVING made their deal with Hitler and Mussolini over the fate of Czecho-slovakia, Chamberlain and Daladier at once faced the question of what to do about Spain. During the opening months of 1939, Loyalist resistance crumbled fast, but even before the Republic finally capitulated, Franco was asking for British and French recognition. He did not get it until the fighting ended.

"EXCUSE ME, BUT DID YOU HEAR A PIERCING SCREAM?"

BY October 10, 1938, German troops and agents had completed the occupation of those parts of Czechoslovakia that the Munich Conference had assigned to Germany. But the process of dismemberment did not stop there. On November 27, Polish troops occupied the little district of Teschen and on November 30 the Czechoslovak National Assembly elected Emil Hacha President of what remained of his country. On March 13, 1939, Hitler summoned Hacha to Berlin and on the same day, Slovakia proclaimed its independence and set up a separate government under the leadership of Father Tiso in the city of Bratislava. On March 15, German troops marched into Prague and Hitler took the Czech provinces of Bohemia and Moravia under his protection.

"A PIECE MISSING, TOVARISH"

ON March 10, 1939, just before Hitler took over all that remained of Czecho-slovakia, Stalin delivered a speech attacking the appeasement policies of the western democracies and warning that the Soviet Union would not pull other nations' chestnuts from the fire. Then, on March 31, Great Britain took the unprecedented step of guaranteeing Poland against aggression. Polish Foreign Minister Beck, who had worked with Hitler in times past, came to an under-standing with Prime Minister Chamberlain but refused to make any conces-sions to the Russians in order to bring them into a wider system of collective security. And Chamberlain preferred to close his deal with Beck and leave the Russians out in the cold.

"...LOVES ME, LOVES ME NOT..."

ON April 7, 1939, Italian troops landed in Albania and five days later King Victor Emmanuel of Italy accepted the Albanian crown. Prime Minister Chamberlain still hoped against hope that he might reach an understanding with Mussolini concerning Mediterranean problems where Italy's expansionist program was becoming a more and more obvious threat to the vital interests of the British Empire.

"WARMONGER!"

ON April 15, 1939, President Roosevelt addressed messages to Hitler and Mussolini asking them to guarantee twenty-seven different countries against aggression. He got a violent response. Hitler not only rejected his proposal, he also took the British guarantee to Poland as the excuse to denounce the Anglo-German Naval Treaty of 1935 and the ten-year non-aggression pact that old Marshal Pilsudski had forced the Germans to sign shortly after Hitler came to power. At that time, the Polish Army could have overwhelmed the Germans and the Germans had no choice but to accept Pilsudski's proposition. Unfortunately, few other European statesmen dared or cared to take so strong a stand.

HOW TO GET A CCLD

ON May 5, 1939, Maxim Litvinov resigned his post as Soviet Foreign Commissar and was replaced by Vyacheslav Molotov who had not identified himself with Litvinov's doctrine of collective security and the indivisibility of peace. Nevertheless, the Russians left the door open to further negotiations with the British, but the Chamberlain government still hesitated. The contacts that Chamberlain maintained with Mussolini led him to hope that he could still come to an understanding with the Axis and reconstruct the Four-Power Pact that had seemed so near at the time of the Munich Conference.

"MIND YER BACK!"

FEW elected public officials in Great Britain wielded more real power during the years between the wars than Montagu Norman, governor of the Bank of England, a private banking organization that had the sole right of issuing British currency and fixing the interest rate. Mr. Norman, a close personal friend of Dr. Schacht, head of the German Reichsbank, had supported and even inspired Chamberlain's appeasement policy and when Hitler took over Czechoslovakia, Norman helped the Germans to acquire the Czech gold reserve. It was also at this time that a group of British industrialists went to Germany and paid the foundations of an Anglo-German agreement to divide world markets between British and German cartels.

"ALL YOU HAVE TO DO IS TO SIT DOWN"

ON June 7, 1939, the British Foreign Office sent one of its permanent officials, William Strang, to Moscow to try to persuade the Soviet Union to join Great Britain in guaranteeing Poland and the western democracies against German aggression. But the Russians refused to make commitments in western Europe unless the British would make similar commitments to guarantee their security in the East. Poland also presented an obstacle. The Poles refused to enter into any agreement that would have permitted Russian troops to enter their country to fight the Germans.

EXPERT ASSISTANCE

RUSSIAN demands for common action against "indirect aggression" also raised an obstacle to Anglo-Russian agreement. The Russians feared German infiltration in the Baltic States and sought British guarantees against German aggression in that quarter, but the British refused on the ground that such action would compromise the independence of these Baltic countries. Meanwhile, the Germans had given a demonstration of indirect aggression in that part of the world when they forced Lithuania to yield the port of Memel. This led to a wry piece of humor in Czechoslovakia which had by that time been absorbed into Germany. "Who would have thought at this time last year," one Czech is reported to have said to another, "that we should now have Memel?"

"But isn't it the Chinese you're supposed to be fighting?"
"Yes, please, but no can beat hon. Chinese."

SOME SORT OF VICTORY URGENTLY NEEDED

EVEN before the war reached Europe, the Japanese took advantage of British difficulties with Germany to push for further concessions from the British in the Far East. During the month after the Munich crisis, Japanese troops had taken two of China s most important cities—Canton in the south and Hankow in central China. Although the Japanese asserted that they sought only to bring law and order to China, they at once placed restrictions on all other foreigners there. The British had permitted the Japanese to take over their concessions in Hankow where the Japanese Army stages what it called a "model occupation." Even so, however, the British found themselves unable to continue any sort of business activity. And the Japanese kept raising their demands.

PRESENT IN SPIRIT

BY July, 1939, the Japanese had placed so many restrictions in the way of foreign trade with China that Britain's Ambassador Craigie undertook a series of conversations with Foreign Minister Arita. Meanwhile British and American oil companies were selling the Japanese the petroleum Japan needed to keep its war machine going and other British and American traders were doing a big business in other war supplies. The Anglo-Americans wanted to have it both ways. They did not want to lose their war trade with Japan. At the same time they also wanted to do business in China on the old basis. Finally, they feared that any embargo of oil shipments to Japan would lead to a war that they wanted to avoid at all costs in view of the threatening situation in Europe.

DREAMLAND FACES THE SITUATION

THROUGHOUT the summer of 1939 until the Nazi-Soviet Pact freed
Hitler to attack Poland and then strike at the west, most of the people in most
of the democracies went through the motions of normal living. The British
refused to meet the Russians half way in Eastern Europe. A majority of the
Foreign Relations Committee in the United States Senate agreed with Senator
Borah that there would be no war in 1939 and rejected President Roosevelt's
plea to amend the Neutrality Act in such a way as to permit quick and large-
scale American aid to the democracies. The Japanese had bitten deep into
China. Hitler and Mussolini were biting ever deeper into Europe. An organized
aggressive minority was calling the tune to which the rest of the world soon
had to dance.

UNCLE SAM'S BOMB-PROOF SHELTER

DURING President Roosevelt's first term, Republican Senators Nye and Vandenberg launched an investigation of the munitions industry which revealed that certain private interests had profited from American participation in the First World War. These revelations led, in turn, to the drafting of a Neutrality Act which President Roosevelt signed in 1937. This Act forbade Americans to ship goods or lend money to belligerent powers. Another measure, the Johnson Act, also forbade Americans to loan money to nations that had defaulted on their war debts. The threat of war during the summer of 1939 led President Roosevelt and Secretary of State Hull to urge some amendments in this Act in order to strengthen the democracies and warn the Axis powers. But the Foreign Relations Committee of the Senate preferred to stand pat.

"IF THE BRITISH DON'T, MAYBE WE WILL"

THIS cartoon appeared on June 29, 1939. It shows that the alert Mr. Low—like many other people in Britain—foresaw the possibility of a Nazi-Soviet Pact, almost two months before the terms of that pact became public. In March, Stalin had warned the democracies that he would not fight their battles for them. In May, Molotov replaced Litvinov as Foreign Commissar. But the Russians still gave the democracies the first chance to come to terms. It was only after prolonged negotiations and refusal of the British and French to meet the Russians' terms that Molotov opened his door and let Ribbentrop in.

O N August 24, 1939, Foreign Minister Ribbentrop flew to Moscow and signed a ten-year Russo-German non-aggression with Foreign Commissar Molotov of the Soviet Union. The Russians, still smarting under their exclusion from the Munich Conference and unable to come to any clear agreement with the western powers, bought time for their own defense by agreeing to remain neutral in the event of German aggression. The Germans, determined not to get themselves caught in a two-front war, reverted to Bismarck's old policy and took out what he once called a "Reinsurance Treaty" with Russia, thus securing for themselves a free hand against Poland or the west. The ideological differences between Communism and Fascism and the open hostility between Russia and Germany in Spain caused widespread consternation, but it all boiled down to old-style, balance-of-power politics.

"YOU MAY HAVE BEGUN MAN — BUT *I*, ADOLF HITLER, WILL FINISH HIM."

UNLIKE the Kaiser, Hitler rarely invoked God in his speeches. At the time he ordered the invasion of Poland, he assumed full, personal responsibility for the decisions he made and though he never claimed divine powers for himself, some of his followers tried to create a new Nazi religion and mythology from which the God of Jews and Christians would be banned. As the war went on, however, Hitler did invoke the name of God, especially when the tide began to turn against the German cause.

NAZI FARMYARD

ON October 19, 1939, the British and French signed a fifteen-year mutual assistance pact with Turkey. This marked the first wartime diplomatic victory for the Allies. The Germans had tried to build an alliance system of their own which would make Eastern and Central Europe largely self-sufficient and impervious to blockade. But Foreign Minister Ribbentrop not only failed to bring any of the neutrals into line; the Anglo-French Treaty with Turkey blocked possible German expansion into the Middle East.

LITTLE WHITE FATHER

WITHIN a month after the Germans invaded Poland, the German and Soviet governments declared that the Polish State had ceased to exist and they divided what used to be Poland between them. On November 1, the Russians then admitted Eastern Poland into the Soviet Union, dividing it into two Soviet Republics—the Western Ukraine and Polish White Russia—after holding plebiscites. At the same time, Red Army troops began occupying military bases in Latvia. The Russian press hinted at protective measures against attack from the west. They appeared to fear the Allied powers. But they really feared the Germans who already began to feel a little uneasy themselves.

Maybe you should grow a moustache, Rib...

THE BISMARCK TOUCH

WHEN Ribbentrop concluded his treaty with Russia he seemed to be following in Bismarck's footsteps and staving off the possibility of a two-front war. But Bismarck never intended to fight Russia. He took out his "Reinsurance Treaty" with Russia because he feared that the German alliance with Austria-Hungary might involve Germany in an Austrian-Russian quarrel. Bismarck had made his alliance with Austria-Hungary because he feared war with France, but he had a high opinion of Britain and sought no advantages in the Balkans. Ribbentrop, on the other hand, had a low opinion of Britain and regarded the Balkans as part of Germany's Lebensraum.

MINE KAMPF

THE early months of the war witnessed a sudden increase in ship sinkings around the British Isles by reason of German magnetic mines. But the British quickly found a protective device against this secret weapon. The Nazis remembered how close the Kaiser had come to forcing the British to their knees during the First World War by the submarine blockade which Admiral von Tirpitz improvised after the fighting had lasted more than a year. But the magnetic mine did not prove so successful as the Germans had hoped.

WAR OF NERVES

THE winter of 1939-40 was the winter of the "phony war," the war of nerves. Hitler made various gestures in various directions and these gestures were sufficient to spread an atmosphere of fear and uncertainty that proved most disastrous in France. The British at this time—as this cartoon shows—did not take Hitler's strength or his threats too seriously. No doubt the British did under-rate Hitler's power. But it was their complete confidence in themselves and their refusal to let Hitler rattle them that did so much to carry them through the dark days that lay ahead.

"SIEG HEIL! HERE COME THE SUPPLIES FROM RUSSIA!"

THE outside world feared that the Nazi-Soviet Pact not only gave Hitler a freedom of action that the Kaiser never enjoyed; it was generally asserted that the Germans would quickly apply their industrial know-how to Russia's vast resources and that the two countries would make an unbeatable combination. Many Germans had always believed that Germany should cultivate the closest possible relations with Russia; this conviction cut across all party lines and ideologies. But it was not a conviction that the Russians shared. The Russians distrusted the western powers, but they feared the Germans. Therefore the Russians made their first wartime arrangement with the country that they feared in order to buy time to prepare for the worst. During this period, the Russians did little to help build up the German war machine. The truth was that there was little they could do.

T H E so-called "winter war" between Russia and Finland caused even more consternation abroad than the Nazi-Soviet Pact. The Russians themselves declared at the time that they attacked Finland in order to acquire certain positions inside Finland that they needed to hold off an Allied invasion. What the Russians really feared—in the light of their exclusion from Munich—was that the western powers and the Germans would compose their differences and join forces in an anti-Soviet crusade. As for the issues between Russia and Finland, the Russians offered the Finns territorial concessions in the north to compensate for the territorial demands Russia made in the south. But the Finns hoped for more outside help than they got—and the Russians miscalculated the popular mood in Finland where they expected a Communist revolt. Instead of winning the easy victory they had expected, the Russians therefore had to bring in some of their crack troops and the war that began in November, 1939, lasted until March, 1940, when the Finns capitulated to the Russian demands.

"NOW, DO ANY OF YOU SWINE WANT TO ASK ANY QUESTIONS?"

ON April 9, 1940, German troops swarmed into Denmark which at once capitulated without resistance. At the same time, German troops landed at Oslo and other Norwegian cities. Major Vikdun Quisling and his Norwegian Fifth Column had opened the door, and the Norwegian army proved no match for the Germans. The Allies announced that they had begun mining Norwegian waters the day before the German invasion—and the Germans seized on that as an excuse for having struck when and as they did. On April 27, Foreign Minister Ribbentrop exhibited documents allegedly taken from captured British officers, purportedly showing that the British had planned to send an expeditionary force to Norway. But the British effort in Norway proved inadequate. The German success, on the other hand, showed that years of planning lay behind the attack.

THE HARMONY BOYS

MUSSOLINI and Stalin had little in common; Franco and Stalin still less. The Communists kept proclaiming their hatred of Fascism as long as the Nazi-Soviet Pact lasted. Nevertheless, the historic record does show that the Communists in many countries did in fact play the German game until Hitler ordered the attack on Russia. In France, they deserted from the Army; in Britain they denounced the "imperialist war;" in the United States they opposed the draft and lend-lease to Britain. To what extent Stalin ever took directives from Hitler is another matter. From August 22, 1939 to June 21, 1941, suspicion of the western powers caused Stalin to follow a policy that yielded more benefit to Germany than it did to Germany's enemies. But Stalin's point was that that policy yielded more benefit to Russia than any other he could have followed at that time.

MUSICAL CHAIRS IN THE BALKANS

THIS cartoon appeared on April 22, 1940, as Hitler's conquest of Norway was rapidly nearing its victorious conclusion. The Germans had gained complete control over the Baltic, invaluable bases on the Atlantic, and sure access to Swedish and Norwegian iron ore. But these were largely defensive positions that gave the Germans a free hand in other quarters, notably the Balkans. The absorption of Austria and Czechoslovakia opened the path to German expansion toward the southeast and gave Hitler cause to hope that he could succeed where the Kaiser had failed in establishing a Berlin-Bagdad railway and making Germany the dominant power in the Mediterranean and the Middle East. But this program meant that Yugoslavia, Hungary, Rumania, Bulgaria, and Greece would all have to go the way of Austria and Czechoslovakia.

REST IN PEACE

A T half past five in the morning of May 10, 1940—the day this cartoon appeared—German troops crossed the borders of Luxembourg, Belgium, and Holland, without warning. The British Army in northern France at once moved into northern Belgium. German parachute troops descended upon Rotterdam. The military defenses of these small countries soon proved as inadequate as their neutrality policies. British troops, for instance, by coming to the aid of Belgium abandoned the stronger defensive positions they had prepared in France and committed themselves to fight a campaign under almost impossible conditions.

ALL BEHIND YOU, WINSTON

ON the same day that the Germans invaded the Low Countries, Neville Chamberlain resigned as British Prime Minister and King George VI asked Winston Churchill, who had served as First Lord of the Admiralty, to form a new government. The next day Mr. Churchill formed a National Government, retaining Chamberlain and Halifax but adding Laborites Attlee, Bevin, and Morrison. The Labor Party had supported Chamberlain's war measures but had refused to hold any offices in his government or accept any responsibility for its acts. Although Winston Churchill took the conventional Tory attitude on domestic and imperial matters, he had constantly attacked the line that Chamberlain had taken in Europe. And Mr. Churchill's famous "blood, sweat, and tears" speech that he delivered on assuming office rallied the whole country behind him.

ON May 15, 1940, President Roosevelt had dispatched a message to Mussolini appealing to him to keep out of the war, but Mussolini sent no reply. He was following events in France. On May 16, German troops passed Sedan. On May 18, Marshal Pétain became Vice Premier. On May 19, General Weygand succeeded General Gamelin as chief of staff. It was commonly believed at the time that Mussolini awaited only a word from Hitler to attack France from the south where the threat of Italian invasion immobilized part of the French Army. But the Germans revealed later that the Italians were proceeding entirely on their own and ignoring or even flouting the advice of Berlin to remain neutral. Mussolini, feeling he had a score to settle with the French and fearing complete German domination of Europe, proceeded largely on his own.

LOOKING IT IN THE EYE

ON May 20, 1940, British troops began evacuating ten of the Channel ports that still remained open in France and Belgium. On May 28, King Leopold of Belgium surrendered his army of 500,000 men to the Germans. The next day the British evacuation of Dunkirk began. All this time, many British units fought heroic holding actions against the Germans who had overwhelming superiority in tanks and planes. The Belgians had relied on neutrality to save them. The French depended on their Maginot Line, but failed to extend that line beyond the territory facing the German border. The Germans therefore by-passed the Maginot Line and then cut it off from the rear.

"STAY THERE! I'LL BE BACK..."

ON May 22, 1940, the British Parliament passed the Emergency Powers Defense Act giving the Churchill Cabinet dictatorial power to re-organize and nationalize industry and to mobilize and allocate labor. "Business as usual" had come to an end. Laborites who had refused to serve under Chamberlain hailed this Churchill move as a "revolution by consent." They assumed that the British people would get their traditional liberties back when the war ended, but they also believed that many of the wartime controls had come to stay.

GIVE US THE TOOLS

THE Germans owed their quick victories in the west to their tanks and armored divisions. The British troops in France had better equipment than the French, but they were outnumbered by the Germans. In the air, the French proved no match for the Germans and in early June, Premier Reynaud pleaded for "clouds of planes" from the United States. The British had the best fighter planes and fighter pilots in the world, but they could not do more than hold the Germans off some of their debarkation beaches. But machines of war cannot be improvised and the long lead that Hitler had built up for Germany during the 1930's could not be overcome once the Germans unleashed their full power in the west.

"WHERE NEXT, MEIN FÜHRER?"

THIS cartoon appeared on June 4, 1940, the day the British completed the "miracle of Dunkirk" when they evacuated 335,000 men and suffered 30,000 casualties in killed, wounded, and prisoners. Paris lay open to Hitler. So—in the opinion of some—did London. But the German armies had moved across France so fast that they had gotten ahead of their own schedule. The British had not only saved most of their army. They still had their Royal Air Force and their Navy. The Germans, on the other hand, needed time to build the bases from which to attack Britain from the air or to launch an invasion by sea. Hitler therefore had almost no choice, after Dunkirk, but to order his armies to strike south for Paris and to postpone the Battle of Britain.

THE ANGELS OF PEACE DESCEND ON BELGIUM

THE Nazi Fifth Column prepared the way for German conquest. Heinrich Himmler's Gestapo then followed up after the military phase of the war had ended. The word "Gestapo" is an abbreviation for Secret State Police (*Geheim-Staats-Polizei*), and Himmler, the top man in the Gestapo, became increasingly important in wartime Germany. During 1940 and 1941 when German Armies were advancing on all fronts, Himmler's men established a systematic reign of terror and looting in the occupied countries. Their principal aim was to kill off all possible leaders of an anti-Nazi resistance movement. They possessed elaborate information about anti-Nazi refugees whom they systematically rounded up, jailed, and murdered along with native opponents of their rule.

"ON TO GLORY — AND WHATEVER WE CAN GRAB"

ON June 10, 1940, the day that Italy entered the war, President Roosevelt interpolated these words into a speech he had prepared for delivery at Charlottesville, Virginia: "The hand that held the dagger has struck it into the back of its neighbor." High German officers who later fell into American hands reported that here, as elsewhere, Mussolini moved without consulting Hitler and even against Hitler's wishes. Mussolini had simply become convinced that the Germans had won the war and he was moving in to get what he could. Some of his apologists even went so far as to assert that Mussolini sent his troops into the south of France in order to spare the French from German occupation. But the French did not welcome the Italian invaders and a handful of French troops made a lot more trouble than Mussolini had expected.

HERE COMES THE BRIDE

ON June 14, 1940, German troops entered the undefended and unscarred city
of Paris. Tanks, motorized divisions, and infantry poured down the Champs
Elysées. On June 16, Premier Reynaud resigned after conferring with Prime
Minister Winston Churchill in France, and Marshal Pétain took over the government. The next day, Pétain appealed to Germany for an armistice. Hitler
then hoped that his quick, complete conquest of western Europe would set
the stage for a general peace settlement that would make Germany the dominant power on the European continent. He therefore studiously avoided taking
a harsh attitude toward the French and in the early stages of the occupation,
German troops showed a "correctness" they had never shown in Poland. On
the economic side, too, the Germans tried to present themselves as the unifiers
of Europe.

"VERY WELL, ALONE"

ON June 17, 1940, the same day that Pétain appealed to Hitler for an armistice, he also turned down Winston Churchill's offer of a merger between the British and French Empires and joint Franco-British citizenship for all Frenchmen and Britons. Meanwhile, Hitler invited Mussolini to Munich to confer about armistice terms for France. Most people in France believed at this time that the Germans had indeed won the war and to most people in other countries, the British cause looked almost hopeless. But Winston Churchill again rallied his people and called upon them to fight on the beaches, in the streets, and in the hills if it came to a German invasion. And President Roosevelt quietly saw to it that the British received a large shipment of American rifles and other equipment left over from the last war.

GHOST TRAIN

ON June 22, 1940, representatives of the French government that Marshal
Pétain had established in Bordeaux signed the armistice terms that Hitler and
Mussolini had drawn up at Munich. With a dramatic touch of revenge, the
Germans made the French sign these terms in the same railroad car at Com-
piègne, in northeastern France, where the German leaders capitulated to
Marshal Foch at the conclusion of the First World War. The three figures in
the lower right hand corner of this picture are Weygand, Pétain, and Laval.

"I GAVE YOU A NICE PLACARD IN EXCHANGE, DIDN'T I?"

NO sooner did the Pétain government make peace with Germany than appeals began to bombard the United States—some urging America to feed the European democracies that Hitler had conquered; others insisting that feeding Europe was playing Hitler's game. The British re-established the blockade they had set up during the last war, but they had to spread their naval forces over a wider area and the regions that Hitler controlled were self-sufficient as far as food was concerned. At first, the Germans simply looted the countries they had overrun. Then they began to exploit the labor of these countries. But what really made the British blockade effective was the refusal of Britain to quit the war. The Germans therefore had to continue maintaining their war machine and even the continent of Europe did not contain enough resources to permit them to do that indefinitely.

IRISH ARGUMENT

THIS representation of Ireland's wartime neutrality cuts deeper than most. Mutual suspicion between the Catholic south of Ireland and the Protestant minority in the north stood in the way of any single policy. German consular officials remained in Dublin throughout the war. The Irish Free State refused to permit the British to use its ports to fight the German submarine menace. During the First World War, Irish Republicans had worked with the Germans. This time, the collaboration did not go so far. Indeed, many Irishmen fought in the British Army and the neutrality of the Irish Free State did give the British the benefit of a good many doubts. But there were numerous occasions, after the fall of France, when a German invasion of Ireland appeared as likely as a German invasion of Great Britain.

HIDE AND SEEK

BETWEEN the Battle of France and the Battle of Britain, Hitler fought a Battle of the Balkans with Stalin. On June 29, 1940, Stalin won the first round of that battle when Rumania, in response to his demands, ceded Bessarabia and northern Bukovina to the Soviet Union. But Rumania was playing the German game, too. On July 1, the Rumanian Council of Ministers renounced the Franco-British guarantee of their country's territorial integrity and announced that Rumania would "follow the new orientation in Europe." But this did not prove a very rewarding policy. On August 31, the Germans forced the Rumanians to cede two-thirds of Transylvania to Hungary—Transylvania being Rumania's chief territorial acquisition after the First World War. A week later, King Carol abdicated and fled the country.

UNEASY NIGHTS IN THE BALKANS

BECAUSE the Russians took over Bessarabia and northern Bukovina from Rumania before the Germans set up their own puppet government there, Stalin seemed to be getting the better of Hitler in the Battle of the Balkans. Stalin also took advantage of German involvements in western Europe to incorporate three hitherto independent Baltic States—Lithuania, Latvia, and Esthonia—into the Soviet Union. Mussolini, on the other hand, was getting nothing at all—and perhaps because he felt the need of asserting himself somewhere launched his disastrous invasion of Greece in October, 1940.

CADGING A LIFT IN THE EAST

FOR three months during the disastrous summer of 1940, Foreign Secretary Halifax launched a half-hearted attempt to appease Japan by closing the Burma Road over which some war supplies had been reaching the Chiang Kai-shek regime at Chungking. Secretary Hull went along with this policy because the Roosevelt Administration attached primary importance to helping the British hold out. It was at this time that pro-Axis feeling reached its height in Chungking. The Chinese had received little but promises from Britain and the United States, and the Russians—who had once helped them against the Japanese—had signed a non-aggression pact with the victorious Germans.

BRITISH CONCENTRATION CAMP

FROM the time that Hitler had come to power until he attacked Poland, the British had admitted thousands of anti-Nazi Germans to their country. A minority of British reactionaries always resented these enemies of totalitarianism, and their fears did have a justification. Hitler had taken advantage of British hospitality toward anti-Nazis to sneak some of his spies into Britain, disguised as enemies of his régime. During the desperate days of the Battle of Britain, the British authorities naturally had to take precautions and the wonder is not that they cracked down so hard on the refugees in their midst but that they treated them so well.

SEPTEMBER 3rd 1939   SEPTEMBER 3rd 1940

THE SIREN! LOOK OUT!

THE first year of war revolutionized British life. The people had not only armed themselves to resist German air attacks; they had re-organized their whole economy. During August, the Germans began stepping up their air attacks on the British Isles and by this time the British people were prepared to meet the test.

IMPREGNABLE TARGET

THE Germans soon concentrated their air offensive on the city of London, launching their first mass night attack on August 22, 1940. On September 8, Marshal Goering took personal charge of the assault. The Battle of Britain reached its climax on September 15 when the Royal Air Force planes, most of them fighters, destroyed 185 German planes, most of them bombers. The Germans made occasional attacks on other cities—notably on Coventry and some of the Channel ports. But the strategy was clear. The Germans calculated that if they could knock out London, Britain could not continue the war.

MUTUAL BENEFIT

ON September 3, 1940, President Roosevelt informed Congress that he had arranged to exchange 50 over-age American destroyers for 99-year leases of British naval and air bases in the Atlantic Ocean. Submarine attacks had cut into Britain's naval strength, and the destroyer had proved one of the most effective enemies of the submarine. Wendell Willkie who was then seeking the Presidency on the Republican ticket approved the destroyers for bases arrangement but criticized the way Mr. Roosevelt had put it through.

"— AND THEN THERE WERE FOUR"

NONE of the belligerent powers forgot the importance of the Mediterranean and the Balkans, even during the summer of 1940. British submarines continued to prowl the inland sea. Hitler, Mussolini, and Stalin extended their influence into southeastern Europe. The head of Stalin can be seen between the trunk and three branches of the palm tree nearest the water.

"HE ASKED FOR PEACE"

THE agreement signed between France and Germany at Compiègne was not a peace but an armistice. According to these terms, the Germans occupied the northern, industrial half of France, including Paris and the major French ports on the Atlantic. Pétain maintained a government at Vichy which had a certain authority in southern unoccupied France. From time to time, Pétain tried to persuade the Germans to replace the stringent armistice terms with a more favorable peace, but nothing came of his efforts. It was part of Hitler's technique, as set forth in *Mein Kampf,* to keep increasing his demands on his victims.

"BOY, YOU DON'T MEAN TO, BUT YOU MAKE A SWELL CUPID"

AFTER the fall of France, Japanese troops moved into the northern half of French Indo-China. This threat to Singapore and the rest of southeast Asia caused Secretary Hull to place an embargo on shipments of American high-octane gasoline to Japan. Thailand, which lies between Indo-China and the Malay States, had come under Japanese domination, too. This advance of Japan into Southeast Asia not only threatened Singapore, it laid the Philippine Islands wide open to attack.

"THE NEW ORDER"

ON September 27, 1940, Germany, Italy, and Japan signed a ten-year pact "to assist one another with all political, economic, and military means when one of the three contracting parties is attacked by a power at present not involved in the European war or in the Chinese-Japanese conflict." But the terms of the treaty did not "in any way affect the political status which exists at present as between each of the three contracting parties and the Soviet Union." This declaration has just one meaning. Japan promised a declaration of war on the United States if the United States became involved in the European war. And Germany promised a similar declaration if the United States became involved in the fighting in Asia.

ORDERS AND DECORATIONS

ON the day this cartoon appeared, October 4, 1940, Hitler and Mussolini held one of their notorious Brenner Pass Conferences at the German-Italian border. Japan had just come more completely into the Axis and Russia was again being isolated, as had happened at Munich just two years before. This was the first of Low's cartoons to suggest that Stalin had become the victim and not the beneficiary of the Nazi-Soviet Pact.

"WAIT, MAYBE I DON'T GO! I AIN'T SO SLEEPY"

BY the middle of October, 1940, when this cartoon appeared, Hitler's plans for Stalin had become more obvious—and so had Stalin's refusal to go along with them. Having failed to break British resistance with air attacks, Hitler shifted his attention to southeastern Europe and the Middle East. This represented a clear threat to Russia. Stalin could perhaps afford to let Hitler control Central Europe, but any extension of German influence to the Dardanelles or to the Middle East threatened Russia with encirclement from the south.

"HELP! HERE'S ONE SHOWING FIGHT!"

THE Germans and the Russians had improved their positions in Eastern Europe during the summer of 1940 and by autumn Mussolini decided Italy should follow suit. On October 26, the Italian news agency announced that "a band of armed Greeks attacked with rifle fire and hand grenades Albanian outposts near Koritza." Since Albania had come under the Italian crown in 1939, Mussolini dispatched a three-hour ultimatum to Athens and when it was rejected Italian planes started bombing Greek cities. On October 28, Hitler and Mussolini conferred at Florence. But the fighting went badly for the Italians. On December 6, Greek troops had taken Porto Edda—the Albanian seaport named for Mussolini's favorite daughter who had married Foreign Minister Ciano—and Marshal Badoglio resigned as Italian chief of staff.

"DEMOCRACY IS JUST A BIG FAKE!"

WENDELL Willkie's campaign for the presidency of the United States caused enormous satisfaction in Great Britain. Mr. Willkie endorsed Mr. Roosevelt's foreign policy, especially his aid-to-Britain program. Of course, most Britons favored the re-election of Roosevelt, if only because the President was a known quantity who—it was said—had come into the war on Britain's side ahead of the rest of the American people. But if Mr. Willkie had challenged Mr. Roosevelt's whole foreign policy, as some of his fellow-Republicans urged him to do, the war might have ended quite differently—even though the election might not.

"WHAT—ME AGAIN?"

THE Italians encountered nothing but grief during the closing months of 1940. Their attack on Greece backfired. On December 10, General Wavell launched an offensive against Marshal Graziani's forces in Egypt and Libya and presently had them on the run. Prime Minister Churchill had made an historic decision. He and his commanders committed the one armored division in the British Army to hold off the Italians from Cairo, Alexandria, and the Suez Canal. The calculation—which proved correct—was that one division more or less could make little difference to the fate of Britain which would be decided on the sea and in the air. But if British troops could hold their own in North Africa, they would not only preserve the Empire but prepare the way for future offensives against what Churchill called "the soft under-belly" of the Axis.

FAMILY GROUP

HITLER'S new order in Europe looked less imposing during the comparative calm that came with winter than it had looked during the violent summer months of 1940. The German Army had given the world an impressive demonstration of military prowess, but when it came to organizing his allies and his victims for any other purpose except destruction, Hitler made a less impressive showing. In 1940, the Germans had the power to do with Europe what they pleased. Not since the sixteenth century and the Holy Roman Empire of Charles V had Europe come so close to achieving unity of a sort. But the very nature of Hitler's program doomed his efforts in advance.

NEW YEAR OUTLOOK

WHEN this cartoon appeared at the end of 1940, the British could look back with pride on a year of unparalleled achievement. After Hitler had overrun all of western Europe, Britain had withstood the air blitz and the German plans for an invasion of the British Isles never got underway. The year 1941 therefore presented new problems to Hitler. Would he continue to hammer at Britain? Would he invade Spain and North Africa? Would he concentrate on trying to create a working new order in Europe? Or would he take the wildest gamble of all and throw his whole strength eastward against Russia?

Isn't that your own little pet
of twelve months ago,
Benito?

OLD FAITHFUL

UNTIL Mussolini delivered his stab in the back to France, he described
Italian policy toward the European war one of "non-belligerence." And it was
a policy that helped Germany more than his active intervention. By 1941, the
United States was pursuing a similar policy of "non-belligerence"—or "steps
short of war"—favorable to Britain. By the end of January, 1941, when this
cartoon appeared Congress had begun to debate H.R. 1776, the so-called
"lend-lease act" which provided for enormously increased war shipments to
the British without any immediate payment of cash on the barrel-head.

"WE BOTH OFFICIALLY DENY THIS IS HAPPENING"

THIS cartoon appeared on February 13, 1941. Two days later Bulgaria joined the Axis and German troops closed in on Yugoslavia from the east and on Greece from the north. The Bulgarians had also entered the First World War on the German side, but this time they had less choice in the matter. Bulgaria is a country of small peasants. It has always looked more to Russia than to Germany for protection, but Bulgaria had also quarreled with most of its Balkan neighbors and the Germans exploited this split in the Balkans to their advantage.

"I WILL BET YOUR *SHIRTS,* TOO!"

HAVING forced Bulgaria into the Axis, Hitler went to work on Yugoslavia. This cartoon appeared on February 19, 1941. A month later the Yugoslav government of Prime Minister Cvetkovich capitulated to Hitler's demands. But within twenty-four hours, General Dusan Simovich executed a coup d'état and established an anti-axis government with the support of young King Peter. The Serbs of Yugoslavia who comprise just over half of the country's population supported Simovich. They remembered how the Austrians and the Germans had treated them during the First World War. The Croats, on the other hand, held back and when German troops invaded Yugoslavia on April 6, the Serbs offered the strongest resistance while the Croats either stood aside or helped the Germans.

THE HONEYMOON BEGINS

DURING the spring of 1941, Foreign Minister Matsuoka of Japan journeyed to Europe by way of Russia. The Germans hoped to bring him closer to the Axis, but the unexpected resistance that the Yugoslavs offered to German penetration of the Balkans put a crimp in Hitler's plans. Matsuoka therefore signed no new agreement with Germany, but on his way home through Moscow he signed a non-aggression pact with Stalin who confounded the Axis diplomats by going down to the railroad station and personally bidding farewell to Matsuoka. By agreeing to respect each others' interests in Asia, the Japanese were free to move south; the Russians free to move west.

"CIEL! CAN'T YOU SEE BY THE FLAG WE'RE FRENCH?"

ON July 3, 1940, British war vessels shelled and sank part of the French fleet at Oran. This led the Pétain government to break off relations with Great Britain. Admiral Darlan, the commander of the French fleet and second in command to Pétain, never forgave this action of the British and worked with the Germans. However, the British did permit some French merchant vessels to pass through their blockade until the spring of 1941, when this cartoon appeared, and Darlan's collaboration with the Germans was arousing more and more antagonism in Great Britain.

HARVEST MOON

EARLY in May, 1941, German air attacks on Britain reached an all-time high. But with the British bagging thirty or forty German planes a night, losses became so severe that the Luftwaffe abandoned its efforts as it had already done once before during the previous autumn. Twice, the Germans tried to paralyze Britain with air attacks and thus set the stage for invasion. Twice they failed. But it was a closer thing in 1940 than in 1941.

"HE MUST HAVE BEEN MAD"

THE end of the air blitz of 1941 against the British Isles came suddenly. It coincided with the flight of Rudolf Hess, Hitler's personal adjutant and number three man in the Third Reich, to Scotland where he landed by parachute. The Germans released several versions of his flight—among them the report that he had gone mad. In 1946, at Nurenberg, Hess revealed that he had made the trip on his own responsibility in the hope that he could persuade the British and the Germans to make peace. He believed that he might persuade King George to fly back with him to Germany and consummate the arrangement with Hitler in person. Ironically enough, it was this story that established Hess's sanity in the eyes of the Nurenberg court to which he told it.

THE FORGOTTEN SENTRY

ON May 12, 1941, two days before this drawing appeared, Admiral Darlan conferred with Hitler at Berchtesgaden about incorporating France into Germany's new order. The Germans were trying to gain special rights from the French in Syria, gateway to the Middle East, and Darlan made secret concessions behind the back of his venerable chief of state. Like many other people in both Britain and France, Low always credited Pétain with a certain sincerity and drew a clear distinction between him and most of the other members of the Vichy government who deliberately and even willingly worked with the Germans.

AWAKE! ARISE!

WITHIN a week after war broke out in Europe, President Roosevelt proclaimed a "limited national emergency" in the United States. Then, on May 27, 1941, President Roosevelt proclaimed an "unlimited emergency." His first proclamation puzzled students of the Constitution which gives the President power to proclaim a "national emergency" but does not draw any distinction between degrees of emergency. But there was no doubt after the President's second statement that a national emergency did exist. He warned of the danger of attacks directed from Dakar in West Africa against Latin America and he also ordered American troops to Greenland which he declared was part of the Western Hemisphere. Later in the summer of 1941, American troops also landed in Iceland as lend-lease supplies flowed in mounting quantities to the British Isles.

SCHOOL'S IN

ON top of the German land invasion of Greece and Yugoslavia came the German air invasion of Crete, where some of the lessons learned in the Battle of Britain were applied. Things looked still worse for the Allied cause. The Germans had not only extended their control over the entire Balkan peninsula; they were reaching out into the Mediterranean. Already German air attacks on merchant shipping in Suez had blocked the Canal to regular traffic; all this was costing Hitler precious time and even more precious equipment and trained men. It was delaying his invasion of Russia by days, weeks—perhaps even months. And it was weakening German striking power when the zero hour finally arrived.

ALI RUBS HIS LAMP

ON June 1, 1941, the Germans had finally completed their conquest of Yugo-slavia, Greece, and Crete. The way seemed open for Hitler to achieve the Kaiser's dream and establish direct, overland connections between Germany and the Middle East. Two obstacles remained to be overcome. First, the Germans needed the support of the Arab world. Second, the Germans needed the cooperation of the Turks whose country lay between the Balkans and the Middle East. The Germans went to work first on the Arabs and in the person of Ali Rashid they found a Fifth Columnist to take over the government of Irak and oust British influence. But British resistance in the Balkans and Crete prevented the Germans from arriving in Irak on schedule.

"HI, JOE! I WONDER IF YOU'D DO ME A FAVOR..."

TURKEY presented an even more serious obstacle to Hitler's march toward Bagdad—and Russia presented the biggest obstacle of all. The Turks who had fought in the last war on the German side persistently clung to their neutrality. They never took the Nazi-Soviet Pact too seriously and believed that the Russians could not afford to let Hitler drive through their country and thus threaten the Soviet Union from the south as well as from the west. And there is reason to believe that Stalin's refusal to make any deal with Hitler in respect to Turkey and the Middle East—as he had done in respect to Poland and Eastern Europe—may have proved the decisive factor in Hitler's decision to attack the Soviet Union on June 21, 1941, one week after this cartoon appeared.

RUSSIAN TREACHERY

WHEN Hitler order the attack on Russia, he and his generals were not the only people in the world who counted on a quick victory. Most military experts in most of the rest of the world expected that the Germans would reach Moscow in short order. But it was also generally assumed that Hitler's decision to invade Russia meant that he could not win the war and would eventually meet the fate of Napoleon. The Red Army then confounded the experts. The pre-war purges had eliminated many opponents of the Stalin regime—including Marshal Tukhachevsky, chief of staff of the Red Army. The winter war in Finland also gave the Russians a chance to bring some of their tactics up to date. And the Germans complained that the Russians had deliberately sent their least efficient troops in Eastern Poland in order to give Hitler a sense of false confidence.

"WHATEVER YOU CALL IT—"

NO sooner had Hitler attacked Russia than Prime Minister Churchill delivered a long-prepared speech pledging that Britain would fight at Russia's side to the end and not make a separate peace with Germany. No single act by any statesman during the entire war did more to dispel Russian suspicions because Churchill himself had violently attacked all the Soviet leaders—including Stalin—from the time of the Russian Revolution until the rise of Hitler. Many Russians could hardly believe their eyes when they read the text of Churchill's address—and even in Great Britain it surprised some circles.

THE FASTER WE GO THE FURTHER AWAY IT GETS

PRESIDENT ROOSEVELT'S proclamation of an unlimited national emergency coming on top of the passage of the lend-lease act on March 11, 1941, reminded the Germans that victory still lay far ahead. Hitler had failed to organize a working new order in Europe. He had lost the Battle of Britain. He had run into unexpected opposition in the Balkans and the Middle East. According to the best evidence General Marshall could get from captured German officers after Germany had surrendered, Hitler never had a definite plan for world conquest. He had counted only on the conquest of Europe in the apparent belief that if he controlled Europe he would also control the world. But this calculation, like many others, proved wrong.

EAST OR WEST?

THE German attack on Russia opened new paths of conquest to Japan. American lend-lease, already flowing to Britain in considerable quantities, started moving toward Russia, too. President Roosevelt re-asserted the doctrine of the freedom of the seas—which the Neutrality Act had denied—and announced that the United States would take steps to see that the goods it was lend-leasing to Britain and Russia reached their destinations—and presently the United States Navy began convoying American merchant vessels across the Atlantic. Thus, German aggression in Europe weakened the Anglo-American powers in the Pacific. The Japanese had just signed a neutrality pact with the Russians. Would they honor that any more than they had honored the Nine-Power Pact supporting the integrity and independence of China?

WRITING ON THE WALL

T H E British soldiers who returned from Dunkirk brought with them the sign of defiance—"Thumbs Up!" By the summer of 1941 a new sign appeared —the V-sign of Victory. Prime Minister Churchill was not the only man who gave this sign wide circulation. Anti-Hitler opposition in Europe had begun to stir and underground fighters made the Germans perpetually uneasy by chalking up the V-sign in unexpected public places. Not only had the German New Order failed to win any popular support outside Germany; Hitler's attack on Russia set the whole Communist movement of Europe into active opposition against the Germans.

"IT'S NOT BRITAIN'S WAR, REALLY. IT'S JUST A WAR TO HELP HITLER TO GET WHAT HE NEEDS TO WIPE BRITAIN OUT."

BATTLE FOR BRITAIN — PART 2

NEARLY everybody in Great Britain thanked God for Russia when the Red Army absorbed all of Germany's striking power during the summer of 1941. The air attacks which abruptly ended with the arrival of Rudolf Hess were not resumed, but as the fury of the fighting mounted and confidence in Russian resistance increased, some of those same Die-Hard Tories, who had always hoped that the Germans and Russians would bleed themselves white fighting each other, began to make themselves heard again.

FISHING TALK

FROM August 9 to August 12, 1941, President Roosevelt and Prime Minister Churchill, conferred aboard the American cruiser *Augusta* just off the North Atlantic Coast. At the conclusion of their conference they issued the 8-point Atlantic Charter committing both countries to certain general principles in any peace settlement that might come. Whereas President Wilson's Fourteen Points covered many specific regions of the world, the Atlantic Charter confined itself to principles only. Never before had the chief of state of a nation nominally at peace issued a common declaration of war aims with the chief of state of a nation that had been at war for almost two years.

"ONE BY ONE" QUEUE

ALTHOUGH President Roosevelt had proclaimed an unlimited national emergency at the end of May and Germany had attacked Russia by the end of June, many Americans still believed in early September, when this cartoon appeared, that the war might pass them by. So far, however, two separate wars were raging on opposite sides of the world. This cartoon covers only the nations that the Germans attacked. But the Japanese had been fighting China for ten years and were preparing to move east and south as well.

"GAD, SIR, WE CAN'T START OFF WITH THE ENEMY'S BACK TURNED. ALL OUR PLANS ARE FOR WHEN THEY'RE FACING US."

WE MUST HAVE THEIR UNDIVIDED ATTENTION

THIS cartoon appeared just three months after the Germans attacked Russia. The Red Army was still absorbing almost the entire weight of the German war machine, and Soviet agitation for a "second front" in western Europe had begun. But already, British die-hards were finding reasons not to prepare for a cross-Channel operation. Throughout the war some British advocates of sea and air power argued that the Royal Navy plus the Royal Air Force could between them bring the Germans to their knees by protracted bombing and blockade.

"WHAT, NO MOSCOW? WELL, BRING ME *THAT*"

THIS cartoon appeared in late October, 1941, more than four months after the Germans had launced their attack. The initial drive against Moscow had lost its momentum. Another was still to come before one of the bitterest winters in Russian history stopped the Germans cold—in more ways than one. Down at the southern end of the front, near the Black Sea, the weather did not present quite such great difficulties. Although the Russians still held the Crimean peninsula, the Germans had driven close to Rostov-on-the-Don and were getting within striking distance of the Caucasus Mountains and their oil fields. But as events developed, that drive had to wait until 1942.

BY the autumn of 1941, the German campaign in Russia and the wind-up of the fighting in the Balkans enabled the British to take the offensive again in North Africa. It is perfectly true—as this cartoon shows—that the Axis troops in Africa did retreat far and fast; the Italians, especially, had little stomach for hard fighting. But it was also true that a desert war is a war of movement. Nature offered little protection against a well-prepared offensive and as a result the battle lines kept shifting back and forth for distances of several hundred miles.

THE ADMIRAL COMES ON BOARD

ON October 18, 1941, Prime Minister Prince Konoye resigned and was succeeded as head of the Japanese government by his war minister, General Tojo. Konoye had tried to arrange for a meeting with President Roosevelt similar to the Roosevelt-Churchill Atlantic Charter meeting, but the evasive attitude of the Japanese during the preliminary negotiations made it clear to Washington that no real agreement could be reached. Ambassador Joseph C. Grew summed up the attitude in Tokyo when he quoted a Japanese diplomat who had said, "How can we compromise when you refuse to accept our views?" The departure of Konoye marked the end of all hope for peace by negotiation —or even by appeasement. The Japanese war party had taken over completely.

"JAPAN PROTEST AGAINST ENCIRCLEMENT! YES—NO?"

IN early November, 1941, when this cartoon appeared, the Japanese had sent Saburo Kurusu to Washington as special envoy to join their Ambassador, Admiral Nomura, in his protracted talks with State Department officials. The Konoye government had already moved troops into southern Indo-China and the United States had retaliated by freezing all Japanese credits and bringing Japanese-American trade almost to a standstill. President Roosevelt had told Prime Minister Churchill at their Atlantic Charter meeting that he thought he could "baby the Japs along" for several months more without war. But Japanese expansion had by this time reached American, British, and Dutch spheres of influence. This led Prime Minister Tojo, who had replaced Konoye in October, to announce that America, Britain, Holland, and China were encircling Japan.

"ALL PRESENT AND CORRECT, MA'AM"

THE Japanese attack on Pearl Harbor quickly established the closest military partnership in history. The United States had already begun to transform itself—in President Roosevelt's words—into the "arsenal of democracy." Immediately after Pearl Harbor, Prime Minister Churchill and his top military advisors journeyed to Washington where they established the Joint Chiefs of Staff with their American "opposite numbers." From that year-end meeting on, Roosevelt and Churchill planned Anglo-American strategy together on a global basis.

SIT DOWN TO IT, LADS

ALTHOUGH the United States and the British Empire set up a Joint Chiefs of Staff to plan a common military strategy immediately after Pearl Harbor, the Chinese continued to fight a separate war against Japan, and the Russians continued to fight a separate war against Germany. But the Roosevelt-Churchill conferences in Washington did lead to a declaration of principles by all the nations then at war with the Axis. President Roosevelt christened this grand alliance the United Nations and the declaration of principles to which all of them subscribed included, among other things, the eight-point Atlantic Charter.

EARLY CHRISTMAS DINNER AT ROSTOV

IN early December, 1941, the fighting in Russia turned for the first time to the advantage of the Red Army. The Germans—thwarted at Moscow and Leningrad—drove into the city of Rostov-on-the-Don down at the southern end of the front. The Russians, who had held the Germans at other vital spots, launched their first successful counter-offensive and recaptured the city from the Germans. Marshal Timoshenko had organized this victory. He was one of the younger Soviet commanders and had replaced old Marshal Buddenny, of revolutionary fame, whose cavalry tactics had failed to stop the German drive in the south.

"IN FUTURE THE ARMY WILL BE GUIDED BY MY INTUITIONS"

ON December 21, 1941, Adolf Hitler took over supreme command of the German Armies from Field Marshal von Brauchitsch. The campaign in Russia had bogged down and the four principal German commanders on the Eastern front were all relieved of their commands—Field Marshals List, von Reichenau, von Runstedt, and von Bock. They had wanted to pull their armies further back. Hitler, however, insisted that his intuitive powers were superior to their military knowledge. When the time came for Hitler to deliver his usual New Year's speech, he admitted that the German war machine had run into its first difficulties. He warned that "still harder battles" lay ahead. Those that lay behind were the most costly in history.

ANOTHER NAZI GENERAL TO BE SACKED?

FROM the moment the Germans attacked Russia, Stalin played a more and more conspicuous role in the conduct of Soviet affairs. First, he assumed the office of Premier whereas heretofore he had contented himself with the position of General Secretary of the Russian Communist Party. In addition, he played an active part in the direction of the war and presently assumed the title of Field Marshal. He proved himself a far more effective military leader than Hitler. Good luck—in the form of good weather—had favored the Nazis in their invasion of France. In Russia, luck and weather turned against them and German troops on the Eastern Front found themselves gripped by the coldest Russian winter in a century—and without regular winter equipment. The German withdrawals that had begun at Rostov, down at the southern end of the front, continued as far north as the front outside Leningrad.

"A TOAST TO THE RED ARMY, RAT!"

THE winter of 1941-42 on top of the heavy campaigning of the previous summer had shattered two military myths: the myth of German invincibility and the myth of Russian weakness. The Russians had sustained heavier losses than the Germans—if only because all the fighting had taken place on Russian soil, and German armies had occupied territories that contained about one-third of Russia's population and industrial resources. Nor had the Germans exhausted their fighting power. The decisive battle of the Russian campaign still lay ahead—at Stalingrad. But the Germans had already suffered a moral setback and the Russians had won a moral triumph that suggested the tide of war had already begun to turn against Hitler.

"SURE, WE'RE PAN-AMERICANS! LOOK, HERE'S OUR PAN"

IN January, 1942, Under Secretary of State Sumner Welles arrived in Rio de Janeiro to represent the United States at a conference of the foreign ministers of all the American Republics. He urged all of them to break off relations with all the Axis powers and on January 21, the conference passed a unanimous resolution to that effect. Brazil and the Central American Republics supported Mr. Welles's stand from the start, but Foreign Minister Guinazu of Argentina hesitated. The Germans still had friends and supporters in Latin America. The Franco regime in Spain had even more. But the pressure for a break with the Axis was too strong and all of them finally supported Mr. Welles.

SPRING ASSIGNMENT

IN the middle of February, 1942, when this cartoon appeared, many people in England found it hard to understand why Hitler's intuition had caused him to invade Russia in 1941 rather than attempt major drives on Gibraltar and Suez first. The German set-backs in Russia and Japan's rapid advances in southeast Asia then led to more speculation concerning a possible Axis drive against the Mediterranean life-line. The German armies had made greater progress at the southern end of the Russian front than at the north. Franco had tied Spain to the Axis and sent troops into action against Russia. No serious obstacle would have prevented the Germans from establishing themselves strongly in French North Africa, especially with the connivance of the anti-British Admiral Darlan. And King Boris of Bulgaria had made southeast Europe safe for Hitler.

INEVITABLE NIGHT

GATHER YE ROSEBUDS WHILE YE MAY

DURING the first months after Pearl Harbor, the Japanese war machine piled up unprecedented conquests in the southwest Pacific and southeast Asia. Japanese planes sank two of Britain's biggest battleships—the *Repulse* and the *Prince of Wales*—three days after Pearl Harbor. Before the first of the year, the Japanese had taken Hong Kong and entered Manila. On February 1, the British abandoned the defense of the Malay peninsula. Two weeks later Singapore fell. The Japanese had also occupied the American islands of Wake and Guam. They were advancing into Burma and the Dutch East Indies. President Roosevelt ordered General MacArthur to leave the Philippines and proceed to Australia and it was there that Allied strategists began planning the first counter-attacks against Japan.

THE arrival of General MacArthur in Australia in March, 1942, boosted Allied morale at a dark time. The United States had already sent some 80,000 troops to Australia and Japanese planes were raiding Port Darwin and other points along the north Australian coast as if in preparation for an invasion. British difficulties in Malaya and North Africa where several Australian and New Zealand divisions had suffered heavy casualties caused the people of those two British Dominions to look more and more to the United States. President Roosevelt met this situation by setting up in Washington a Pacific War Council composed of high officials from Britain, China, Canada, Australia, New Zealand, and the United States who held weekly meetings—often with President Roosevelt—to co-ordinate the Pacific war.

STRAIN ON THE TAIL

BY the end of March, 1942, when this cartoon appeared, the Japanese had occupied New Guinea and virtually completed their conquest of the Dutch East Indies. General Stilwell was taking what he later called "a hell of a beating" as he led a small doomed army of Allied soldiers out of Burma. At this point, Japan's war strategists had the choice of driving in a southeasterly direction toward Australia or in a northwesterly direction toward India. The long lines of supply prevented them from bringing a heavy concentration of power to bear. They also lacked the men and material to wage war on the scale the Germans did. Therefore they did not move decisively anywhere. But they gave the southwest Pacific more attention than India—and according to correspondents with General Stilwell lost a golden opportunity to invade India.

AT the end of March, 1942, the British Government sent Sir Stafford Cripps to India with an offer of independence or dominion status at the end of the war on the condition that the Indian people could reconcile their differences and get behind a single government. Until then, India was to support the British war effort and contribute more heavily to checking the Japanese. Sir Stafford Cripps used to favor Indian Nationalism; he was an old friend of Nehru, one of the leading figures in the Indian Congress Party. But some of the Congress Party leaders suspected any British offer and even Nehru felt that the British had left themselves an out by insisting on unity within India before making any further concessions. The Japanese were also appealing to the Indians with the slogan "Asia for the Asiatics"—and Sir Stafford returned to Britain empty handed.

AWAITING THEIR CHANCE

DURING the dark days of 1942, a Japanese attack on Russia always seemed an imminent possibility. Many persons believed that the Japanese attacked Pearl Harbor only because they believed that the Germans could not be prevented from taking Moscow. Later, captured German officers declared that the fall of Stalingrad was to serve as the signal for a Japanese attack on Russia's rear. Although some Americans had already begun to demand that Russia open a "second front" against Japan in Manchuria—or at least provide Siberian air bases for American flyers, the Russians pursued what eventually proved to be a wiser policy. They kept enough troops in Siberia to immobilize many of Japan's best divisions—and the chance for which these divisions were waiting never came.

MAY I WALK INTO YOUR PARLOR, SAID THE SPIDER TO THE "FLY"

THE man who had preceded Hitler as German Chancellor and had prepared the Nazis' path to power received an important wartime assignment. During the First World War, von Papen had abused his diplomatic privileges in the United States where he had served with the German Embassy until the United States government forced his recall. Before the Second World War, Hitler appointed him Ambassador to Austria where he schemed against the Republic in behalf of the Nazis. Then, in 1942, with all the rest of the Balkans under control, Hitler appointed von Papen Ambassador to Turkey. He is shown here with King Boris of Bulgaria under his protection. Von Papen was such a tricky character that even the Nazis distrusted him and he was lucky not to have been liquidated during the purge of June 30, 1934.

SLIGHTLY BLIND IN THAT EYE

AFTER the British had shelled the French fleet at Oran early in July, 1940, the Pétain government broke off relations with Britain but neither party ever declared war. The British did, however, encourage General DeGaulle to organize his Free French movement in London while President Roosevelt maintained contact with the Vichy regime by sending Admiral Leahey there as his personal ambassador. Meanwhile, Vichy authorities continued to exercise authority on the little Caribbean island of Martinique where the French aircraft carrier, Béarn, lay interned. British Liberals and the Laborites used to scold Secretary Hull from time to time because he appeared too friendly toward Vichy, but there was no disagreement at the top. Washington was playing the Pétain side of the street; London was supporting DeGaulle. Between them, the Anglo-American powers were keeping as many contacts with as many Frenchmen as possible.

THE SQUEEZE PROCESS

LIKE almost everybody else in wartime Britain, David Low regarded Pierre Laval rather than Marshal Pétain as the real villain of the Vichy set-up. It was Laval rather than Pétain who arranged for the shipment of Frenchmen to Germany as slave laborers. Laval also enriched himself during the occupation and in December, 1940, Pétain asserted himself to the extent of dismissing Laval as Prime Minister, but the Germans presently forced Laval back into office and, through him, tightened their grip on France. The Germans not only squeezed labor power from France; they wrecked the French economy by issuing worthless currency, charging excessive occupation costs, and expropriating French industry with the connivance of a few French supporters of the Vichy régime.

"WHAT NEWS FROM THE SECOND FRONT?"

ON May 12, 1942, the German armies launched a two-million man offensive against the southern Russian front. The Russians held and even counter-attacked at Rostov-on-the-Don—down at the southern end of the line—and at Kharkhov, further north. But the Germans threw the main weight of their initial drive against the Crimean peninsula and the great port of Sevastopol. The Russians had already suffered heavy losses; their resistance had given relief to Britain. The United States remained unscathed by war. The Russians felt that the Anglo-Americans had sufficient time and resources to launch an invasion of Western Europe large enough to force the Germans to shift at least sixty divisions from the east. The agitation for the second front had begun.

"HEY, YOU—CHURCHILL! THIS WAS MY IDEA!"

ON the night of May 30, 1942, more than a thousand British bombers attacked the German city of Cologne in the largest single air raid in history. At the outset of the war, Goering, as commander of the German Luftwaffe, promised that no foreign planes would drop any bombs on any German city. A sudden burst of optimism followed. It was not generally recognized at the time that the British had made extraordinary preparations for this attack and had put almost every available bomber into the air. Also, the outside world did not yet know how quickly and thoroughly the Germans learned to protect themselves and their industries against attacks from the air. But it marked a formidable beginning of what later became one of the decisive battles of the war—the battle for control of the air over Germany. The Anglo-Americans also began to argue, with increasing insistency, that these air attacks on Germany were becoming the equivalent of a Second Front.

"NOW SUPPOSING WE ALL TRY TO GO
SOMEWHERE TOGETHER..."

DURING the month of June, 1942, Foreign Commissar Molotov visited Washington where President Roosevelt issued a statement recognizing the "urgency" of opening a second front that year. The British had already signed a 20-year friendship treaty with the Russians. But the Anglo-American Joint Chiefs of Staff still planned the global war while the Russians and the Chinese concentrated on their own immediate problems. As the summer continued, the hope that an over-all United Nations or Big Four High Command might be established grew dimmer. In July, the Anglo-Americans definitely decided against an invasion of Western Europe. Correlation of strategy had to wait.

NOW FOR SOME TEAMWORK, JOE

FOREIGN Commissar Molotov was the first high Soviet official to establish personal contacts with the Anglo-American leaders. Two months after Molotov visited London and Washington, Prime Minister Churchill visited Moscow and conferred with Stalin. He had a tough assignment. The Joint Chiefs of Staff had decided against the invasion of western Europe in 1942 and most Russians believed that the Anglo-Americans had broken the pledge that President Roosevelt appeared to have made in June. But in spite of the blunt, harsh speaking that marked this first Churchill-Stalin meeting, the two men did at least get to know and respect each other.

IN OCCUPIED TERRITORY

THE very ease with which Hitler's armies moved through Europe seemed to augur success for his New Order. The Germans found few enthusiastic collaborators, but they met with little opposition from the pre-war governments. During the summer of 1940, the Germans had a real chance to prove that they could succeed where the governments that they had routed had so clearly failed. But the Germans quickly kicked away whatever chances they had. Their doctrine of racial superiority and their systematic looting of all the countries they overran stimulated resistance and an increasingly powerful underground movement developed everywhere. The Germans then adopted still more ruthless methods, with Heinrich Himmler's Gestapo steadily extending its powers. And many Germans—like Hitler in this cartoon—still could not understand why Europe did not accept them at their own valuation.

"THOSE WHO BITE OFF MORE THAN CAN CHEW SUFFER DENTAL DISFIGUREMENT."—

WISDOM OF THE SOLOMONS

DURING the spring and summer of 1942, three battles turned the tide of the Pacific War. In May, the Japanese sent a large fleet into the Coral Sea, headed for Australia. American naval vessels and American Army and Navy planes sank 100,000 tons of Japanese shipping and saved Australia. A month later, the Japanese sent a large task force of battleships and carriers against Midway Island. American planes brought down 275 Japanese planes and sank or crippled ten Japanese battleships, cruisers, and carriers and damaged three Japanese transports. On August 7, the United States Marines landed on Guadalcanal Island in the Solomons, thus launching the first Allied offensive since the Japanese had struck at Pearl Harbor exactly eight months before.

SUBSTANCE AND SHADOW

THE British had never offered so many concessions to India as Sir Stafford Cripps proposed when he went on his famous mission early in 1942. And, for a time, there seemed a real chance that the Indian leaders might accept the offer which would have given them the choice of Dominion status, freedom within the empire, or complete independence—*after* the war. But the British insistence that the Indians must first agree among themselves led to the rejection of the offer, and in the summer of 1942 the Indian Congress Party, acting on Gandhi's instructions, ordered a campaign of civil disobedience for the purpose of gaining complete independence at once. Although Jawaharlal Nehru favored stronger resistance to the Japanese than Gandhi called for in his non-resistance program, he nevertheless supported the civil disobedience campaign with the result that he and Gandhi and other Congress Party leaders were jailed by the British early in August, 1942.

"MORE!"

THE great German offensive launched by Marshal von Bock on the south Russian front during the summer of 1942 looked more dangerous than anything the Germans had done in 1941. On July 2, the Crimean port of Sevastopol fell, and soon afterward German troops had overrun the rest of the Crimean peninsula. Other German troops had also driven across the River Don and raced to the banks of the Volga and the foothills of the Caucasus. Some Russian oil wells fell into German hands. But the Russians fought stubbornly and forced von Bock to pour in more and more reserves. Finally, in September Stalin ordered the Red Army to hold the city of Stalingrad, on the west bank of the Volga at all costs, and the decisive battle of the Russian war began.

IN THE PAGES OF HISTORY

T H E Russian stand at Stalingrad stands out as *the* decisive battle of the Second World War. It was here that the Russians finally broke the offensive power of the German army. It was here, also, that the Russians themselves faced their greatest crisis. If the Germans had been able to hold Stalingrad and drive on across the Volga, they could have swept up on Moscow from the south; the oil wells of the Caucasus would have been doomed; the stage would have been set for the Germans and the Japanese to link up together, perhaps in India. The battle of Stalingrad began in September, 1941. The Russians held all through October, though some German units did reach the banks of the Volga. In November, the Russians counter-attacked. On January 1, 1943, the Russians announced that they had surrounded twenty-two German divisions in Stalingrad, killed more than 300,000 German troops in six weeks, and would annihilate all the Germans in South Russia.

RELEASE OF
FRENCH PRISONERS
THIS YEAR – NEXT YEAR
SOMETIME – NEVER

INDUCEMENT TO INFAMY

WHEN Marshal Pétain signed the armistice with Germany, the Germans held some two million French prisoners of war. From that time on, the Germans kept using these prisoners to force more concessions from the French, but they released only a small proportion of them and always received French workers in exchange. Nearly all the French war prisoners held by the Germans were men in the prime of life. The Germans hoped by retaining these prisoners to cripple France permanently. The low French birth rate fell still further and the French war prisoners in Germany lived under such bad conditions that many of them could never again expect to regain their normal health and vitality. The Germans looked far ahead. Even if they could not win the Second World War, they wanted to eliminate France as a great power.

HOW MUCH FOR THIS LOT?

GERMANY'S armies could never have driven deep into Russia and occupied most of Europe without the support of German industry, and German industry could never have supplied these armies without a large and docile supply of labor. Dr. Robert Ley, the leader of the German Labor Front, therefore, had one of the most important German war assignments: it was his job to man Germany's factories—and since most able-bodied Germans were in uniform he had to recruit some eight or ten million slave workers from the occupied countries. In Pierre Laval, Dr. Ley found a willing collaborator, all the more so because Laval liked nothing better than to line his own pockets at other peoples' expense.

PINCER MOVEMENT

ON October 25, 1942, General Montgomery issued an order of the day telling his British Eighth Army to destroy General Rommel's Afrika Korps. On November 7, Allied troops—most of them Americans—under the command of General Eisenhower began landing at Casablanca, Algiers, and Oran. Prime Minister Churchill had already committed the British to the defense of Egypt. Britain therefore lacked the troops to launch an invasion of Western Europe. President Roosevelt insisted that some American troops should see action against the Germans before the end of 1942. The landings in North Africa offered the logical solution and the Axis, for the first time since 1939, found itself gripped in an Anglo-American pincer.

"ARE YOU GOING HOME FOR CHRISTMAS THIS YEAR?"

DURING December, 1942, the Russians began to report their first large-scale victories. They had not only turned back and annihilated the Germans at Stalingrad; the Red Army surged forward along more than half the entire front—all the way from Rostov-on-the-Don up to Moscow. The German retreat became a rout. The Russians advanced as much as thirty miles a day and they estimated German casualties at 80,000 killed or wounded. The Russians also picked up enormous stores of German war equipment—a million shells, more than 2,000 guns and mortars, 6,000 trucks. The tide had turned—and in the words of Winston Churchill "the end of the beginning" had come.

"MAKE ROOM—YOU'VE GOT COMPANY"

AS soon as Wendell Willkie returned from his trip around the world at the end of 1942, he began his campaign for world unity that culminated in the publication of his book, *One World*. At first he warned chiefly against any exclusive Anglo-American attempt to seek exclusive post-war advantages. Mr. Willkie had visited both Stalin and Chiang Kai-shek and he pointed out that the Soviet Union and China would play a much greater part than they ever had played before and that the age of empire in Asia had come to an end.

**BROTHER HANS, BROTHER HANS, DO YOU SEE
ANYBODY COMING?**

THE North African landings took the Germans so completely by surprise that the Allies went ahead much faster than they had anticipated. General Eisenhower was a commander who believed in taking chances. He therefore ordered General Anderson's First British Army to drive for Tunis and it made rapid progress during the early weeks. The few Germans in Tunis feared that Hitler would not be able to supply help in time—and it was a close thing. But General Anderson ran into some difficult country; he had a long supply line; and the Germans did manage to rush some reinforcements across the Mediterranean by sea and air.

—AND WE STILL DON'T BELIEVE IN SANTA CLAUS

WHEN the Allied Armies landed in North Africa, General Eisenhower tried to establish contacts with French leaders who would rally the local population to the Allied cause. General DeGaulle's Free French movement had little support among the French officers and French colonial officials in North Africa. Nearly all of them hated the Germans, but they also respected Marshal Pétain. By pure chance, Admiral Darlan who was second in command to Pétain, appeared in Algiers when the Allies landed and in return for his co-operation, General Eisenhower recognized him as commander of all the French forces in North Africa. Many people in England resented this decision because Darlan had taken a conspicuously anti-British attitude and there was a good deal of criticism in the United States too. But President Roosevelt and Prime Minister Churchill backed General Eisenhower's judgment—and on Christmas Eve a young Frenchman shot and killed Darlan in Algiers.

"THERE, SEE! SOME PEOPLE DO GET CHRISTMAS PRESENTS"

WHEN the Allies established air bases in North Africa, their medium bombers and fighters began to operate in the air over Italy. Italian morale had already suffered badly as a result of the defeats in Africa and the war had long ago failed to yield the benefits Mussolini had promised. Most Germans regarded most Italians with contempt; most Italians hated the Germans. But there was little the Italians could do in their own behalf, and in so far as the Germans attempted to defend Italy against air attacks, they concentrated on those parts of Italy that were vital to the German war effort.

QUOTH THE EAGLE, "NEVERMORE!"

ALTHOUGH General Eisenhower failed to take Tunis quickly and had to plan a long campaign in North Africa, the Germans stood to lose either way. By deciding to stand and fight in Africa, the Germans lost 110,000 men; the Italians 40,000. Rommel's Afrika Korps retreated all the way to Tunis and the German Luftwaffe took its first bad beating since the Battle of Britain. Although the Allies had to maintain a long supply line, the North African campaign proved far less costly to them than it had to the Germans. It also gave the untried American troops battle experience that stood them in good stead in the Italian campaign and the invasion of Western Europe.

CHINESE PATIENCE ON A MONUMENT

DURING the latter half of 1942, the tide of the fighting in the Pacific turned against Japan. The battle for Guadalcanal developed into one of the closest, costliest, and most protracted battles of the Pacific War. The United States Navy suffered its most costly losses since Pearl Harbor. United States Army troops finally relieved the United States Marines who had held on against heavy odds. At the same time in the western Solomon Islands General MacArthur's forces had reached the northern coast of New Guinea. By the end of the year, the United States had not only won the battle for the Solomons and thus secured bases to continue the offensive, Japanese losses in the land, sea and air fighting far exceeded American losses. But from General Stilwell who commanded all the American forces in China came these words: "We are doing our best in our small way to try to crack a hard nut. It would be easier if we had more tools, but we are the last stop on the line."

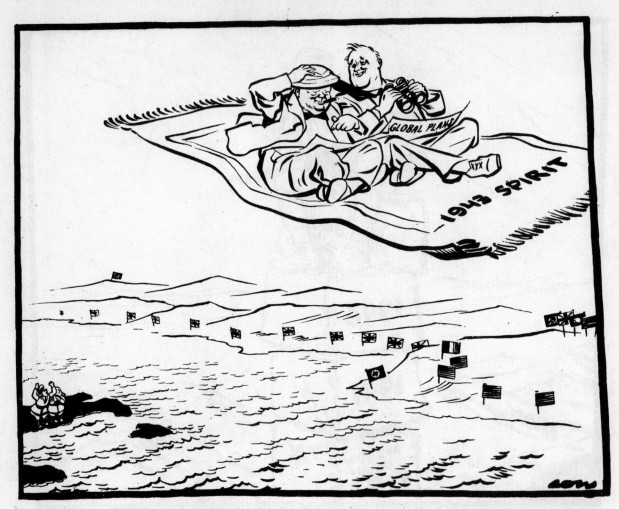

FLYING STATESMEN

BARELY two months after the successful Allied landings in North Africa, President Roosevelt and Prime Minister Churchill both flew to Casablanca with their top military advisers to plan more global strategy. It was at a news conference in Casablanca that President Roosevelt first used the words "unconditional surrender" which at once became the definition of Allied war aims. Premier Stalin had also been invited to attend the Casablanca meeting, but he said he had his hands full directing the Russian winter offensive. And the failure of the Anglo-Americans to invade Western Europe in 1942 still rankled.

CHANTICLEER GREETS THE DAWN

FOR a short time, the Casablanca conference appeared to have established unity among all Frenchmen fighting the Axis. The murder of Admiral Darlan removed a troublesome figure. President Roosevelt had no difficulty in bringing General Giraud to Casablanca as the new supreme French commander in North Africa. Giraud had escaped from a German prison and had never held office under Vichy. But his conservative background alienated him from General DeGaulle's more radical supporters. Also General DeGaulle wanted to keep a tight personal control over the Free French movement. Prime Minister Churchill had great difficulty in persuading DeGaulle to come to Casablanca and carry out the gesture of shaking hands with Giraud. But President Roosevelt added his pressure and DeGaulle consented to go through the necessary motions.

"I'VE SETTLED THE FATE OF JEWS"—"AND OF GERMANS"

DEFEATED in Russia and North Africa, thwarted in his plans to establish a New Order in Europe, Hitler increased the fury of his attacks on the Jews in occupied Europe. But there was more than blind frustration behind the German mass murders of European Jews. The Nazis had planned to liquidate certain races, to make others into slaves, and to concentrate all power and privilege in the hands of a Nordic minority. Nazi degenerates and fanatics carried out the program, but it had a definite and wider purpose and for that reason the sins of the Nazis were visited upon the German people.

"WHAT ABOUT US, MR. MACMILLAN?"

AFTER the Allied Armies had liberated North Africa, they found that the French had interned many thousand Spanish Loyalists who had fought against the troops of Hitler, Mussolini, and Franco from 1936 to 1939. This cartoon, which appeared on February 26, 1943, was directed to the attention of Harold Macmillan who had become the chief British diplomatic representative in North Africa.

FLAME THAT WON'T BLOW OUT

AS soon as the Allies invaded North Africa, Hitler ordered his armies to occupy all of France. The Vichy government broke off relations with the United States and Pierre Laval assumed more and more power while Marshal Pétain faded into the background. But the French resistance movement took a new lease on life. French naval officers ordered their fleet at Toulon scuttled and went to their deaths on the bridges of their vessels rather than turn them over to the Germans. French resistance fighters made their way in ever-increasing numbers to North Africa and to the British Isles. The Allies supplied them with arms. German repression only fanned the flame of revolt.

FASTER! FASTER! THROW OUT MORE ITALIANS!

ON March 31, 1943, the day before this cartoon appeared, General Montgomery's Eighth British Army broke the so-called Mareth Line that the Germans had established in southern Tunisia. Rommel's 1,750 mile retreat across the African desert had entered its last lap and the toll of Italian prisoners mounted fast. Most of these Italians had no more stomach for fighting. In addition, the Germans were running short on supplies and feared that their crack Afrika Korps would be caught between the Eisenhower drive from the west and the Montgomery drive from the east.

"HI! YOU CAN'T DO THAT THERE 'ERE"

WHEN Germany overran Poland in 1939, a group of Polish officials made their way to London and set up a Polish Exiled government there. A trickle of Polish soldiers followed and some of them joined the Royal Air Force and helped win the Battle of Britain. When Germany attacked Russia, the Russians released hundreds of thousands of Polish soldiers, some of whom joined the Red Army while others trained separately and made their way to the Middle East under the command of General Anders. By this time, General Sikorski— a Polish patriot of unimpeachable integrity—had become head of the Polish Exiled government, had visited Stalin, and gained Russian recognition for his régime. But General Anders and most of the other Polish Exiled leaders continued to snipe at Russia while they also warred on Germany.

THE WEDGE

DR. Joseph Goebbels scored one of his major triumphs of the war during the early months of 1943 when the German radio broadcast the report that German soldiers in Russia had found the corpses of 10,000 Polish officers, allegedly killed by the Russians in Katyn Forest. Day in and day out, the German radio had disseminated similar stories purporting to show friction among members of the Grand Alliance that had finally seized the initiative in the war against the Axis. But this particular story fell on fertile soil. Many of the exiled Poles wanted to believe the worst of the Russians—and the honest historian must admit that Goebbels had a ready-made tradition of hatred and fear to exploit. The Exiled Polish government in London at once rose to Goebbels' bait and demanded that the International Red Cross investigate the Katyn affair. The Russians replied by breaking off relations with the London Poles.

RATS

THEY have them in England, too. Before the shooting war began, they hoped that the Germans and the Russians would bleed each other white while the rest of the world remained at peace. Then they proclaimed the Nazi-Soviet Pact an "unholy alliance" through which Hitler and Stalin would divide the world. When the Germans attacked the Russians, they predicted that Moscow would fall in three weeks and that Hitler would knock Russia out of the war by 1942. But when the Russians held firm at Leningrad, Moscow, and Stalingrad, a new obsession appeared: the obsession that Stalin would dominate the world as Hitler never had.

SHAKY WAY BACK

ON May 7, 1943, the day this cartoon appeared, American troops under General Eisenhower took Bizerte and British troops under General Montgomery entered the nearby city of Tunis. The African campaigns had ended in sudden and complete disaster for the Axis. Free French troops had gone into action as well as the troops of General Giraud. Allied planes had shot down more than 500 Axis planes with a loss of 175. This Allied air offensive had also extended to Italy. The great bulk of the German and Italian armies in North Africa never did escape across the Mediterranean. Instead they surrendered unconditionally. The Allies announced that in two years of fighting in North Africa they had taken about 400,000 prisoners and had wiped out eleven German and twenty-six Italian divisions.

"NOT YOU, BONZO! GO HOME, SIR!"

AS the Germans prepared to defend Italy against an Allied invasion, the Nazi Party sought the support of the Vatican. Hitler had sent as German Ambassador to the Vatican an old-line German diplomat, Baron von Weiszacker, but Hitler had not forgotten that Pope Pius had refused to endorse his invasion of Russia as a crusade against the godless Bolsheviks. Nor had the Pope forgotten the Nazi anti-Catholic record, especially in Poland and in other predominantly Catholic countries in Eastern Europe.

Image labels: MUMMY-CASE of the poor old *WORLD-REVOLUTION POLICY* DIED ABOUT 20 YEARS AGO — DMITROV — ZHDANOV — BUSINESS AS USUAL — STOOPIDS OF THE WESTERN WORLD — LOW

COMINTERMENT

ON May 21, 1943, Premier Stalin announced the liquidation of the Third Communist International—or Comintern. The leaders of the Bolshevik revolution had organized the Third International to supersede the Second Socialist International and during the years between the wars the Communists had built up a world-wide organization. But after Stalin ousted Trotzky, the Comintern devoted itself more and more to the promotion of Russian national interests and soft-pedalled its earlier propaganda for world revolution. By the time Germany attacked Russia, the Comintern had become more of a liability than an asset and as Russia's leaders came to believe more and more in permanent cooperation among the major powers fighting the Axis they finally decided to put the Comintern out of business. George Dmitrov, the Bulgarian Communist who headed the Comintern, had taunted Goering at the Reichstag fire trials. Zhdanov held a leading position in the Russian Communist Party and stood especially close to Stalin.

"ITALY WILL NEVER SURRENDER," SAYS BERLIN

A S General Eisenhower's Allied armies in North Africa prepared to invade Italy, Allied planes dropped messages to the Italian people urging them to turn against the Germans and surrender. "The Italy we used to know and love" —as Low calls it—did still exist, but it could not speak for itself or take much action against the Germans. Mussolini had committed himself entirely to Hitler and through him the Fascist Party continued to keep the Italian people in line. During the month of June, Allied air power forced the Italian garrison on the little Mediterranean island of Pantelleria to surrender and the moment for the first Allied landings on the European continent was at hand.

"DON'T ANYBOD' WANT-A TO FIGHT-A FOR *ME*?"

AT the height of his power, Mussolini had identified himself with the glory that was Rome, but as the inevitable end drew near, his prestige melted away. The Italian people had never accepted Fascism as the Germans accepted Nazi-ism. At most, the Italians regarded Fascism as another and not very appealing manifestation of a national tradition that has expressed itself in many forms during the past 2,500 years. Carlo Scorza, secretary of the Fascist Party, therefore made no mention of Mussolini in his last, desparate appeals —and Mussolini, always a physical coward, had little energy left even to fight in his own behalf.

WHAT! ANOTHER ONE?

ON June 5, 1942, a revolt of Argentina Army officers ousted the legal government of Acting President Ramon Castillo. Illness had incapacitated President Ortiz, and the strong pro-Axis forces in Argentina took the opportunity to strike. They operated under a smoke-screen because General Rawson who led the military revolt enjoyed an anti-Axis reputation and the outside world was informed that the change had purely domestic significance. But within a few days after the new government came into power and had received recognition, General Rawson was forced out by General Ramirez who, in turn, was the creature of Colonel Juan Peron, the real power behind the revolt. Even under Castillo, Argentina had failed to carry out its pledges to the other American Republics under the Rio de Janeiro Conference of January, 1942, and remained the one nation in the New World that had not broken relations with the Axis.

"MARE NOSTRUM"

ON July 10, 1943, Allied troops landed on the island of Sicily and on July 19 American planes bombed military targets in Rome. On July 25 a split inside the Italian Fascist Cabinet forced Mussolini to quit, and Marshal Badoglio became Prime Minister in his place. German agents quickly spirited Mussolini away to northern Italy where he proclaimed an Italian Fascist Republic, but his power over the rest of the country had gone and his new régime in the north amounted to nothing more than a collection of puppets, manipulated by the Germans. Marshal Badoglio insisted that Italy must be defended as a single unit or get out of the war, but it took him and the Royal House of Savoy more than a month to make up their minds what to do.

MAKE YOUR MINDS UP

THE final Italian surrender came on September 8, 1943, five days after Allied troops crossed the Messina Straits from Sicily and landed on the toe of the Italian boot. Marshal Badoglio recognized little King Victor Emmanuel as his sovereign and the Allies dealt with them as the only representative government then functioning on Italian soil. Although plenty of Italian anti-Fascists wanted to fight on the side of the Allies against the Germans, the chief anti-Fascist strongholds lay in the industrial centers of the north where the Germans had dug themselves in deep. The people of southern Italy are primarily very poor peasants—except for the big city of Naples which had lagged behind the rest of the country in accepting Mussolini and which also moved slowly in accepting the Allies.

"WHAT—NO ADMITTANCE FOR (AHEM!) SYMPATHIZERS?"

ONE of the most important conferences of the entire war took place at Quebec in August, 1943, when President Roosevelt, Prime Minister Churchill, and their top military advisers finally agreed to launch an invasion of Western Europe in 1944. Hitler's satellites now saw the writing on the wall and sought in vain for admission. Stalin, who would have been welcome, still held aloof. But the decisions reached at Quebec prepared the way for the first Big Three meeting at Teheran. Foreign Minister T. V. Soong of China attended some of the Quebec sessions and new plans were made to defeat Japan. Four areas of command were more strictly defined: Admiral Lord Mountbatten in Southeast Asia; Generalissimo Chiang Kai-shek in China; General Douglas MacArthur in the Southwest Pacific; and Admiral Nimitz in the northern and central Pacific Ocean.

BE CAREFUL TO
FIX THEM SO THAT
THEY CAN TURN
BOTH WAYS

DEFENSE OF THE NAZI HOME FRONT

THE sudden collapse of Fascism in Italy caused the sharpest moral crisis of the war behind the German lines. Invasion of the Reich still seemed far away, but the Russian Armies were moving ahead and Allied air attacks were bringing the war home to the German people. During August, 1943, a succession of 1,000-plane raids wrecked the great port of Hamburg. Goebbels at once ordered the evacuation of Berlin to begin. A single raid on Nurenberg left 40,000 persons homeless. The British alone dropped almost twice as great a weight of bombs on Germany during the second quarter of 1943 as the Germans had dropped on Britain during the three heaviest months of the Blitz. Early in August, the last German offensive in Russia had failed and the Russians surged through Orel, on the central front, and into Kharkhov in the south.

BASIC WINSTONESE

THE Allied successes during the summer of 1943 made the chances for a Second Front look up. The German repulse of a large-scale commando raid at Dieppe in August, 1942, had cooled some of the popular enthusiasm for an immediate cross-channel operation, but a year later the picture had changed. The only action that the British Army had seen since Dunkirk had taken place in Africa and civilians and men in uniform were all feeling restless and eager to get on with the war. But Prime Minister Churchill's strategy of attacking Europe first from the south had prevailed and the Second Front had to wait.

IMITATION THE SINCEREST FLATTERY

DURING 1943, German propaganda struck a new and much gloomier note than the German people had heard during the early years of the war. It began with the Stalingrad disaster when German radios spent three days in early February playing dirges and mourning the heavy loss of life on the Eastern Front. Dr. Goebbels also tried to exploit President Roosevelt's unconditional surrender formula by asserting that it meant annihilation for the German people. The new line worked well. Perhaps it was because the German people felt that this time the Nazis were speaking the truth and that dark days lay ahead. Perhaps it was because the Germans respond readily to the propaganda of gloom.

FIRST ARRIVALS AT MOSCOW

IN October, 1943, Secretary of State Hull made the first airplane trip of his life to confer in Moscow with Foreign Secretary Eden and Foreign Commissar Molotov. The three men came up with by far the most comprehensive, hopeful, and specific statement of war aims that had yet appeared—and the Chinese Ambassador to Moscow added his signature to what was at once called the Four-Power Moscow Declaration. In this document the four chief nations at war with the Axis pledged themselves to support a post-war system of world security, backed by force. The Moscow Declaration made such a favorable impression in the United States that Congress inserted some of its phrases in the so-called Connally Resolution, endorsing American participation in a world league to enforce peace.

DNIEPER BEND

THE Germans had concentrated their most powerful offensive of the war on the southern end of the Russian front during the summer of 1942. The Russians struck back in the same region with their most powerful counter-offensive which liberated the great cities of Kiev and Kharkhov. Some of the hardest fighting took place along the wide curve of the Dnieper River which flows into the Black Sea. It was here that the Germans had overrun some of Russia's richest coal mines, hydroelectric plants, and industrial centers. This way also lay the road to the oil fields of Rumania.

YOUR MOVE, TOJO

HAVING driven the Japanese from Guadalcanal and the rest of the Solomon
Islands, the United States Marines moved north and west. On November 20,
1943, they landed with the heaviest proportional losses in military history
on Tarawa in the Gilbert Islands. General MacArthur's troops had already
taken Lae and Salamaua on New Guinea and on December 26, American
troops landed on Cape Gloucester in New Britain. The Japanese regarded
these moves as directed against their great southwest Pacific naval base on
Truk where they were husbanding a large part of their fleet. But the Allies
were pursuing an island-hopping strategy. They did not try to take every
objective in their path but constantly by-passed the Japanese, carrying out
the old baseball maxim of "hit 'em where they ain't."

TWO'S COMPANY BUT THREE'S MORE COMFORTABLE

IN December, 1943 when this cartoon appeared, the Czechoslovak exiled government in London signed a mutual assistance pact with the Soviet Union. The Polish Exiled government also wanted to sign a treaty with the Poles, but the Russians insisted that none of their small neighbors could enter into bilateral agreements that might, conceivably, be turned against the Soviet Union. The Polish Exiled government and the Soviet government had broken off relations earlier in the year and mutual suspicion prevented Poland from coming into an agreement including both Russia and Czechoslovakia.

SPANISH SERENADER

EVEN before Franco won the Spanish Civil War, he had built up considerable support throughout Latin America. Operating through an organization known as Hispanidad, Fascist-minded Spaniards maintained close contact with Latin American governments—notably those of Argentina and Bolivia. Franco's friends in Latin America not only worked for Franco; they worked for Hitler, too, with whom Franco remained on good terms throughout the war. From Latin America, the Germans secured information on Allied ship movements. Latin America also served as a convenient financial clearing house for the Axis powers. But as the war went on, Britain and the United States put more and more restrictions in the way of Spanish infiltration of the Western Hemisphere.

"WHOSE SIDE ARE YOU ON — THEIRS OR OURS?" — "MINE"

AS the year 1944 began, Red Army troops crossed the borders of pre-war Poland. The Moscow radio at once announced that the frontiers Russia had drawn through Poland in 1939 would have to stand. This ran close to the so-called Curzon Line that the British had suggested as the proper Russian-Polish boundary after the First World War. In 1939, the Russians had already incorporated this region into the Soviet Union in the form of two new Soviet Republics—the Western Ukraine and Western White Russia. But the Polish Exiled government wanted all the territory that had belonged to Poland at the time of the German attack and insisted on the so-called Pilsudski Line as the proper Russian-Polish border.

"DON'T FRET CHIEF—I KNOW MY WAY HOME"

BY January, 1944, when this cartoon appeared, North Africa had been liber-
ated for more than a year but the liberation of France still lay six months away.
The French in North Africa had favored Pétain more than DeGaulle; the
French in France preferred DeGaulle to Giraud as their leader. The Allied
authorities had moved slowly—working first with Darlan, then with Giraud.
But this played into DeGaulle's hands, especially as more and more Frenchmen from France made their way to North Africa and worked out plans for
D-Day. DeGaulle not only had great strength in the French resistance move-
ment; he quickly dominated a provisional French Assembly, set up in Algiers,
with representatives from France as well as from North Africa. Indeed, De-
Gaulle sometimes tried to play such a dominant role that more and more
Britons and Americans began to fear he might develop a dictator complex of
his own.

THEY HAVE ONE IN MOSCOW, TOO

FOREIGN Secretary Eden used the words "heritage of suspicion" to describe the difficulties that prevented closer relations between the Russians and the Anglo-Americans. Low has drawn many cartoons depicting the danger of British suspicions of Russia and, since he knows Britain well, he has no difficulty putting his finger on the sore spots. Russian suspicions of the Anglo-Americans arise from various sources. Before the war, the Russians thought mostly of the foreign intervention in their civil war and of the conflicts between Communism and capitalism. But as victory drew nearer, the growth of Russian wartime nationalism gave rise to another kind of suspicion. This was not the revolutionary fervor of the old-time internationalist but the patriotic fervor of the new-style Russian nationalist.

NEW DANCE FROM ARGENTINA

SECRETARY Hull and Foreign Secretary Eden came in for a lot of criticism because of their attitude toward the pro-Axis government of Argentina. Having recognized the new government in the first place, when it had an anti-Axis front, Secretary Hull thought better of his decision and withdrew the American Ambassador. The British took parallel action but maintained their close economic ties. Former Under Secretary of State, Sumner Welles, criticized the Hull policy on the ground that it violated our pledge of non-interference in the internal affairs of Latin American nations and would only strengthen Ramirez. And British Liberals and Laborites criticized Eden for not cracking down more severely. The main trouble in both Washington and London was not too much or too little appeasement; the main trouble was indecision, born of the urgency of the war situation as a whole.

**"HI, YOU! IF YOU WON'T CONSIDER ME,
THINK OF THE LITTLE ONES"**

EARLY in 1944 when this cartoon appeared, Britain and America launched the full force of their growing air power against Germany and the occupied countries of Europe. Some of the accounts of some of these attacks gave rise to the hope that air power alone might win the war. The bombs rained down on the just and the unjust; on collaborators and resistance fighters. German propaganda—like Italian propaganda just before Mussolini fell—soft-pedalled its boasts about Hitler's New Order and German supremacy. Now the Germans tried to pose as the defenders of Europe against three non-European powers: Britain, Russia, and America.

"ARGENTINA? SI, SI, MEIN FUHRER...YOU'RE THROUGH"

ALTHOUGH the Germans were losing ground fast on the Eastern Front while Allied air attacks were bringing the war to the heart of Europe, Hitler still had two important and loyal supporters abroad: Generalissimo Franco of Spain and Colonel Juan Peron, the strong man of Argentina. Germany no longer received much material aid from either Spain or Argentina, but these two countries provided Hitler with two strategic listening posts from which he received information about Allied war plans.

"WHAT, NO RED CARPET?"

BY early March, 1944, when this cartoon appeared, Russian armies were closing in on Finland. In mid-January, the Russians had opened their winter offensive at the northern end of the front when they attacked in the Leningrad area. Finland's participation in the war on the German side had enabled the Germans to isolate Leningrad. It had also given the Germans air bases from which their planes attacked British and American convoys on the northern run to Murmansk. The British, who had declared war on Finland, associated themselves with the Russian surrender demands, but President Ryti, Prime Minister Tanner, and Baron Mannerheim—commander in chief of the Finnish armies—insisted on continuing the hopeless fight.

SOLID BASIS

AT the end of November, 1943, Roosevelt, Churchill, and Chiang Kai-shek met in Egypt and issued their famous "Cairo Declaration" pledging themselves to fight to the end against Japan and to liberate all territories that the Japanese had taken "by fraud and by force." Korea was to receive its independence "in due course;" China was to get back Formosa, the Pescadores Islands, and Manchuria. After Roosevelt and Churchill had completed their talks with Chiang—for whom his wife acted as interpreter—they flew on to Teheran for their first meeting with Stalin.

TRIAL GROUPING

ON November 25, 1943, Field Marshal Smuts, the Prime Minister of South Africa and the senior statesman of the British Empire delivered a speech in London proposing that Great Britain organize a bloc of west European powers to counterbalance and offset Russia's dominating position in eastern Europe. He warned that the end of the war would leave only two world powers —the United States and the Soviet Union—and he therefore suggested that Britain increase its influence in western Europe. Immediately after Smuts spoke, Roosevelt, Churchill, and Stalin met at Teheran where they made their final plans for the defeat of Germany and made their first tentative arrangements that gave Russia a dominating position in eastern Europe but that did not give Britain any corresponding advantages in the west.

WINDING UP

THE Teheran meeting led to quick action. Within a month, General Eisenhower had been appointed Supreme Allied Commander in charge of the projected invasion of Western Europe with General Montgomery in charge of all ground forces. General Eisenhower and most of the commanders who had worked with him in the Mediterranean moved their headquarters to Great Britain where they at once began their plans for D-Day. During the early months of 1944, the mounting air attacks received the widest attention in the news. But all the time the Army Service Forces were piling up the vast stores of equipment necessary for a successful landing on a hostile coast.

DE-PARTISANS

WITH Allied armies advancing up the Italian peninsula and with Russian armies entering Rumania and threatening the Balkan peninsula, the partisan movement developed considerable strength in northern Italy, Greece, and Yugoslavia. King Victor Emmanuel tried to pose as an anti-Fascist. King George of Greece appealed to his royal British cousins and pointed out that he had remained faithful to the Allied cause. Young King Peter of Yugoslavia also recalled that he had sided with the Serbs who had fought the Germans most bitterly when they invaded his country in April, 1941. But some of these monarchs had doubtful pasts; others had unreliable associates. History had passed them by. They had no more influential friend than Prime Minister Churchill, but nobody held them up to more effective ridicule than Mr. Churchill's loyal compatriot—David Low.

FAMOUS LAST WORDS: "GIDDUP!"

BY the end of April 1944, when this cartoon appeared, the Russian winter offensive had cleared all Germans from the pre-1939 territories of the Soviet Union. Russian troops had penetrated the Baltic States in the north; Poland in the center; Rumania in the south. Finland, however, still refused the Russian surrender terms and the Red Army was preparing to move across Lake Ladoga, just above Leningrad, where the Finns had helped the Germans bombard Leningrad for more than a year.

THE CARE OF DOVES

ALTHOUGH Hitler knew that the spring of 1944 would eventually witness an Allied attack on his so-called "Fortress of Europe" from the west, the Russians' offensive posed a more immediate threat. This offensive also worried the pro-Axis governments of Hungary, Rumania, and Bulgaria. Rumanian and Hungarian soldiers had fought side by side with the Germans against the Russians, and the Rumanians hed re-asserted their control over northern Bukovina and Bessarabia which they had ceded to the Russians in 1940. At the same time, Hungary had acquired most of Transylvania from Rumania. The Russian offensive threatened both these countries more immediately than it threatened Germany and their governments had no choice but to stick with Hitler to the end. The Bulgarian government had let German troops into its territory but had never sent any of its troops to fight in Russia. Indeed, Bulgaria and Russia remained at peace.

"—AND WE DIDN'T RUIN THE RUINS, EITHER"

ON June 4, 1944, two days before D-Day, Allied troops entered Rome. The Germans had left the city undamaged. Allied planes had concentrated their attacks on the railroad yards. The bitterest fighting had occurred at some distance. The Allies had expected to break through Monte Cassino to the south and to go ahead quickly from the beach-heads they had established at Anzio to the southwest. But the Germans put up surprisingly heavy resistance and both sides suffered heavy casualties. It took the Allies exactly four months—from January 25 to May 25—to make junction between their forces at Anzio and the forces that had attacked Monte Cassino. But once contact had been made, Rome fell in short order.

CONGRATULATIONS FROM ONE WHO KNOWS

ON June 6, 1944, less than one hundred days after General Eisenhower arrived in Britain, he took the supreme gamble of the Second World War and ordered the invasion of Western Europe to begin. It meant putting more than 3,000 planes in the air and more than 4,000 ships to sea. For two years, the Russians had waited impatiently for D-Day and when it came they expressed satisfaction. But the Russians never did understand the factors that caused such a long delay. The Germans had attacked their country by land. The Russians struck back on the land and their land armies were approaching German soil at the time the Western Allies were landing their troops on the Normandy beaches. But the Western Allies had to send their entire invasion by sea. They had to land on the hostile coast of an enemy-held continent. And General Eisenhower had bet everything on one roll of the dice. If the D-Day landing had failed, there was no telling when, if ever, victory would have come.

A CASE OF RECOGNITION

NO sooner did the Allied Armies land in France than the question of recognizing General De Gaullè began to take care of itself. For several years, the British and the Americans—but especially the British—had been running small arms and ammunition into France, and the French underground had helped hundreds of British and American aviators to escape from the clutches of the Germans and return to the British Isles. This long period of collaboration quickly paid dividends, especially in the Allied invasion from the south where the French Forces of the Interior went into action on a large scale.

CRACKING THE NUT

ON June 19, 1944, less than two weeks after D-Day, the Germans started shooting their first pilotless planes—or flying bombs—against Great Britain. For a few days, the British made light of this new weapon which the Germans called a V-1, or Revenge Weapon Number One. Fighter planes knocked down many of the flying bombs, but more and more got through as the Germans stepped up their attacks. The V-1's cost little to make; they cost nothing in the way of human lives. The pre-invasion air offensive had put all the sites out of commission, but it did not take the Germans long to get them going again and with Allied troops pouring ashore in Normandy, most of the available air power was needed to support the extension of the first beachheads. Allied planes continued to hammer at the "flybomb sites," but it wasn't until ground troops moved in that the rain of V-1 weapons on London came to an end.

PIECE OF CAKE

A S soon as Allied troops landed in Normandy, the Russians lived up to their end of the Teheran Agreement and opened what proved to be the final offensive of the war on the Eastern Front. The first big victory came on June 26 when Vitebsk, near the center of the line, fell. On July 3, the Russians took the city of Minsk, close to the pre-war Polish border. By the middle of July, the Russians had entered Latvia, they were threatening East Prussia, they had taken the ancient Lithuanian capital of Wilno, the Germans evacuated Pinsk—their last stronghold in eastern Poland—and five Russian armies were pointing for Warsaw and Berlin.

GARE DE
CAEN

"OI! GIMME A FIRST-CLASS SINGLE TO PARIS, VITE!"

AT the same time that the Russians were breaking through the center of the eastern front and menacing Warsaw and Berlin, Allied troops cracked German resistance in Normandy. On July 9, British troops took Caen; on July 18, American troops took St. Lô. From then on the German defeat became a rout. General Patton's armored forces streaked across France with nothing but air power to protect their southern flank and they kept on going until they ran out of gasoline near the German border. Allied planes had smashed all the bridges across the Seine with the result that Allied ground troops quickly overran northern France. On August 15, Allied troops landed on the southern coast of France between Nice and Marseilles. They moved ahead faster than General Eisenhower's men had moved into Europe from the west, but they encountered less opposition. On August 25, the German commander in Paris surrendered to the French.

"THIS IS WHERE WE CAME IN . . ."

THE rapid progress of the Allied forces in the west and of the Russian forces in the east suggested that the history of 1918 was about to repeat itself in 1944. But events turned out differently. In August, 1918, Field Marshal von Hindenburg told the Kaiser that Germany could not win the war and urged that peace be made as soon as possible. In July, 1944, many German generals saw Germany approaching a similar disaster. But Hitler was committed to a last-ditch fight. The unconditional surrender formula left no avenue of escape for any Nazi leader—and Hitler believed right up to the end that the Russians and the Western Powers would fall out before Germany collapsed entirely.

..."All human value lies in personality, every idea every accomplishment is the result of one man's creative work and admiration for greatness is not merely a thank-offering paid to it, but also a bond uniting those who are grateful for it."......

LOW

"MEIN KAMPF" RE-READ

ON July 20, 1944, Hitler and his regime barely survived the greatest crisis since the blood purge of June 30, 1934. A large number of German generals, believing that Hitler had hopelessly lost the war, hoped to save something by surrendering as Germany had surrendered in 1918. Because the ambition of Hitler and the plans of the Nazi Party stood in their way, the generals therefore tried to assassinate Hitler himself—and the attempt very nearly succeeded. One general came to a conference with Hitler carrying a time bomb in a brief case. A last-minute misadventure prevented the bomb from killing the Fuehrer and the conspiracy was soon exposed. Hitler remained the supreme commander but Himmler took more and more open control of the home front and a few generals continued to direct the details of the fighting. Hitler went into the shadows for a while.

Victory was so certain even a short while ago that we can prepare ourselves with fresh courage for a later fight....(an) unavoidable fresh contest for the leadership of the world.— *HITLER'S LATEST*

"WILL YOU TAKE MY IOU?"

IN mid-September of 1944 when this cartoon appeared, the British and American people were not alone in expecting that the war in Europe might end that year. Germany had begun the war with air superiority, a large submarine fleet, and more and better armored divisions than any nation. But after the Russians had launched their final offensive from the east and after the Allied armies had swept across France, the Germans appeared to be facing total defeat. Several factors kept them going longer than most Germans probably anticipated themselves: Hitler's determination to fight to the end; the V-1 and V-2 weapons that were creating more havoc in Britain than the blitz; and the last few reserves that were not thrown into the scales until the end of the year.

DUMBARTON ACORN

DURING the late summer and early fall of 1944, delegations from Britain, Russia, China, and the United States held a series of conferences at Dumbarton Oaks, Virginia, to draw up plans for a projected world security organization. First, the original Big Three powers conferred and reached agreement on most points. They planned to rely much more on force than the League of Nations did; they also concentrated more power in the hands of a few big countries. But the Russians insisted that each one of these big countries should be able to veto any action against itself. The British and American delegations did not take so extreme a view and the matter was held in abeyance for the next Roosevelt-Churchill-Stalin meeting to come to some final compromise. The negotiations among the British, Americans, and Chinese went more smoothly.

STUDY IN SELF-RESTRAINT

DURING the 1940 Presidential campaign between Roosevelt and Willkie, most people in England showed a clear preference for Roosevelt but at the same time gave Willkie great credit for endorsing Roosevelt's foreign policy. When Governor Dewey ran on the Republican ticket in 1944 it was a different story. Governor Dewey had opposed Administration foreign policy in 1940. He also conducted a more heated campaign than Mr. Willkie had. But any expression of sympathy for Mr. Roosevelt from any foreign source might have boomeranged and it was with difficulty—and not always with success—that the British tried to conceal their real preference.

SINKING SUN

ONE of the decisive naval battles in history began on October 23, 1944, in Leyte Gulf, just west of the Philippines. American troops had made their first Philippine landings on the central island of Leyte on October 19 and the Japanese threw a large part of their remaining fleet into action. Admiral Halsey's massive Third Fleet and Admiral Kinkaid's smaller Seventh Fleet—popularly known as MacArthur's Navy—hit back. Taking many chances, the two American fleets repulsed and routed the Japanese in a four-day series of engagements. The Japanese lost two battleships, four carriers, and nine cruisers. From then on their Navy ceased to be a factor in the Pacific war.

WATER JUMP

I T was not until the Allied Armies reached the approaches to the Rhine that their steady advance halted. A formidable water barrier confronted them. German garrisons held on to several French ports for months. Le Havre did not fall until September 13; not until several weeks later was the port of Antwerp cleared of Germans. At the end of September, British Airborne troops made a desperate bid to seize the Dutch city of Arnhem and turn the Siegfried line from the north. The failure of this gamble made a long winter campaign inevitable.

WE MUST CONCEAL... IT IS FORBIDDEN TO DISCUSS.... NO DOUBTS MUST BE EXPRESSED...—*says GÖBBELS*

"NOW IF WE CAN ONLY FIND SOME WAY TO STOP THEM THINKING—"

AFTER the plot on Hitler's life had failed, Gestapo chief Himmler and Propaganda Minister Goebbels tightened their controls over the German home front. Allied air attacks were pulverizing Germany's cities. While Allied troops were sweeping across France toward the German border, Russian troops were over-running Rumania and driving across Hungary toward Budapest. On August 24, Rumania surrendered unconditionally. On September 19, Finland dropped out of the war. On October 20, Russian troops entered East Prussia while American troops were completing the occupation of Aachen— the first major German city to fall into Allied hands. This succession of reverses stunned the German people and Himmler had less difficulty than this cartoon perhaps suggests in preventing the Germans from thinking. But few Germans had any doubts about the outcome of the war. By the end of 1944, they knew all was lost and simply went on going through the motions.

WHERE IS HITLER? — THE MYSTERY SOLVED

SINCE the July 20 attempt on Hitler's life, the whereabouts of the German Fuehrer remained a mystery. But on December 16, Field Marshal von Rundstedt who commanded all the German armies in the west, made the final German gamble of the war. He threw 15 divisions through the Ardennes Forest at the center of the Allied lines. This attack not only forced General Eisenhower to order General Patton to wheel up from the south and attack the German southern flank; the attack itself seriously threatened the port of Antwerp—and with it the whole Allied position in northwestern Europe. But the gamble failed. American troops, surrounded in the Belgian city of Bastogne, held on. Patton halted the German advance at the southern side of the bulge. Field Marshal Montgomery who had been given temporary command of all ground forces to the north was equally successful there. The Germans had squandered their last reserves in the west.

BRITAIN LIBERATES GREECE

DURING the month of October, 1944, Prime Minister Churchill visited Moscow where he and Stalin divided the Balkans into British and Russian spheres of influence. Russian troops had already entered the Rumanian capital of Bucharest and Churchill agreed that Russian influence should predominate in Rumania, Hungary, and Bulgaria. They agreed to a 50-50 split in Yugoslavia and British influence was to predominate in Greece. As the Germans pulled out of Greece in October, the British moved in, but on December 1, civil war broke out when the Greek resistance movement—known as the EAM —and the Greek resistance fighters—known as the ELAS—refused to surrender their arms to the British. Presently British troops were firing on Greek partisans who had fought the Germans for three and a half years. On Christmas Churchill and Eden arrived in Athens where they patched up a settlement.

"DER EASTERN GATE ISS STILL CLOSED TO DER ENEMY!"

SOME of the hardest fighting on the Eastern Front occurred in the region around Budapest. The Hungarian capital itself made a natural fortress and the Germans kept on fighting in its streets from late December to early February. It was more than Budapest that was at stake. The Germans attached almost as much importance to the defense of Vienna as they did to the defense of Berlin. Ludendorff and other German military strategists believed that the key to the defense of Central Europe lay in the region between Budapest and Lake Balaton, some 150 miles to the southwest.

MOBILE CANTEEN

THE American Presidential election of 1944 kept Mr. Roosevelt busy and at home during one of the most active periods of the war. But soon after the returns were in Prime Minister Churchill called for a new Big Three meeting "at the earliest possible moment." The Teheran Conference of a year before had set the military strategy which had already paid off and which caused the major allies to pursue a temporary policy of regional responsibility. The British at once ran into difficulties in Greece. The Russians were having trouble in Poland where part of the population supported the Exiled government in London while others rallied to the liberation committee that the Russians had helped some of their Polish friends to establish at Lublin. In this cartoon, David Low expressed a feeling that was widely prevalent in Britain—and in the United States, too—that if the Big Three did not get together soon, the post-war world would divide itself into old-fashioned spheres of influence.

"HAVEN'T YOU GOT SOMETHING IN BETWEEN?"

THIS cartoon, appearing on January 1, 1945, summed up the most important
issue confronting the world at the start of the New Year. A United Nations
victory was by now a foregone conclusion. The Big Three and the lesser
powers had successfully pooled their military resources. But the Teheran
Conference with its emphasis on big power domination and regional responsibility was setting a different post-war pattern from the one that President
Roosevelt and Prime Minister Churchill had outlined in the eight points of the
Atlantic Charter. Most people in most countries probably wanted a program
that would combine the universal qualities of the Atlantic Charter with the
practical advantages of an understanding among the major powers on whom
the main responsibility for peace had to fall.

PEP TALK TO THE DEAD

HITLER opened the New Year with one of the gloomiest broadcasts of his career, delivered from a subterranean hide-out somewhere in Germany. It was gradually becoming apparent that many of his leading military commanders had participated in the assassination attempt of July 20. He still talked of victory, but he no longer suggested that Germany could conquer Europe—much less the world. It had now become, he declared, a battle for the right of the German people to exist. And the Nazis had held power so long that their fate had become the fate of all the rest of Germany too.

"JUST LIKE OLD TIMES"—WITH A DIFFERENCE

AFTER von Rundstedt failed to reach any important Allied objective at the time of the Ardennes offensive, Germany faced total defeat. Not only had von Rundstedt used up his last reserves, Russian troops were closing in on Warsaw and the air offensive over Germany had all but destroyed the Luftwaffe. The Germans still had several million soldiers in the field, but air attacks kept their transportation system in a constant state of chaos, and a succession of air attacks on their synthetic oil refineries hit them in their weakest spot of all.

LIGHTING UP

DURING the darkest hours of the war President Roosevelt held out hope to the British people. It was to President Roosevelt that they again looked as victory drew near. They remembered that the American people had turned away from Woodrow Wilson after the First World War and they hoped that this time President Roosevelt could succeed where President Wilson had failed.

"HI! THIS IS NO TIME FOR FANCIES IN THE FIRELIGHT"

BOTH President Roosevelt and Prime Minister Churchill had to warn the American and British people that the victories of 1944 did not mark the end of the war. Although the German counter-offensive in the Ardennes Forest failed and allied air power and Russian ground troops were attacking Germany on all sides, the German soldiers fought as fiercely as they had at any stage of the war. More young, untrained men had come into the ranks, but they still had experienced officers and non-commissioned officers to lead them.

YOU SAID IT, BUD

ON January 9, 1945, two days before this cartoon appeared, General MacArthur made good on the promise he made when he left Bataan in 1942: "I will return." Troops of the Sixth United States Army landed at Lingayen Gulf on Luzon, the main island in the Philippines, 100 miles north of Manila. The first American landing on the Philippines had taken place on the central island of Leyte on October 19 where General MacArthur established his first headquarters and where President Osmeña re-established the government of the Philippine Commonwealth.

"YOURS, I THINK"
"NO, YOURS"
"OURS"

BY the middle of January, 1945, when this cartoon appeared, Allied counter-attacks had broken the German assault on the Ardennes Forest. General Eisenhower had put Field Marshal Montgomery in charge of American troops along the northern end of the German salient; General Bradley remained in command of those to the south. There were rumors at the time that Montgomery felt he had been slighted when General Bradley was put in command of the largest Army Group on the Western Front and that Montgomery had expected to retain his original position as commander of all the ground forces. But after the battle of the Ardennes had ended, General Eisenhower restored all the American armies to General Bradley's command while Field Marshal Montgomery returned to his original northern sector.

POLAND

TRAIL OF THE BEAST

MARSHAL Zhukov's First White Russian Army captured Warsaw on January 17, 1945, the day before this cartoon appeared. The Germans had made one of their most desperate stands of the war in the Polish capital which had already suffered terrible destruction in 1939. Every single building in the city had suffered some damage. Most of them had been reduced to rubble. A premature uprising of Polish Patriots, acting under the instructions of the Polish Exiled Government, had added to the havoc. The Germans had done their utmost to annihilate the Polish people as well as the Polish state and the ruins of Warsaw stood as a monument to their destructive purpose.

MODEL: "If we only had good communications we could send them our spare panzers"

RUNDSTEDT: "If we only had spare panzers"

ELASTIC DEFENSE

ON January 22, 1945, the Russians avenged themselves for one of the great German victories of the First World War. Where Hindenburg had routed Russia's Rennenkampf in 1914, Zhukov routed Model in 1945. During the closing months of 1944, the Allied offensive in the west had made more rapid progress than the Russian offensive in the east. In fact, the Allies had driven deeper than the Russians into Germany. But in January, the Russians opened their winter offensive in earnest and Allied air attacks on German communications made it impossible for the Germans to shuttle their dwindling armies from west to east and from east to west.

"WHAT HON. ASS CALLED IT THE FORGOTTEN ARMY?"

ON THE ROAD TO MANDALAY

THE crescendo of the fighting on the Western Front riveted the attention of most people in England on the war against Germany. And Americans were dividing their attention between the Pacific War and the fighting in Europe. Meanwhile in Burma, General Slim's Fourteenth British Army—including many Indian troops—had driven the Japanese from eastern India and were gradually pushing down toward Mandalay, Rangoon, and Singapore. This campaign received so little attention that the troops who fought it, under the most difficult conditions, became known as "the forgotten army." And the SEAC (the South East Asia Command of Admiral Lord Louis Mountbatten under whom they fought) became known as the Supreme Example of Allied Confusion.

"We Germans are answering with ringing laughter" — SAYS GÖBBELS

SILLY OLD "BIG 3" AND THEIR ADVICE TO THE GERMAN PEOPLE

LAUGH! DAMN YOU, LAUGH!

THIS cartoon appeared on February 8, 1945, the day after Roosevelt, Churchill, and Stalin opened their five-day conference at Yalta to work out plans for the treatment of occupied Germany and liberated Europe. Goebbels had laid such stress on the disasters that would overwhelm Germany in the event of an Allied victory that he suddenly struck out on a new propaganda line and pretended that the plans of the Big Three left the German people convulsed with laughter. But the retreating soldiers at the front and the bombed civilians in the cities knew different.

"PST! YOU BUY PRETTY POSTCARD, MISTER?
ANTI-RUSHY, VERY MUSHY"

T H E Yalta Conference ended on the day this cartoon appeared—February 12, 1945. President Roosevelt had come by boat and plane from the United States and returned with by far the most detailed and comprehensive agreement that the Big Three ever reached. As he said at the time, some of the Yalta decisions would reveal themselves as events developed, but the Conference produced two major results. First, the Big Three agreed on a common policy toward Germany. Second, they drew up the so-called "Yalta voting formula" whereby the major powers could veto any action against themselves in the projected world security organization but whereby the smaller powers had a chance to present their points of view. Generalissimo Franco was still trying to make Hitler's last, desperate hope come true and create a split in the Big Three.

POLISH DIPLOMACY

PRESIDENT Arciszewski of the Polish Exiled government in London—with the support of most of his colleagues—objected to the Big Three decisions at Yalta, but Prime Minister Mikolajczyk could see no hope for Poland except through collaboration with Russia and the United Nations on the terms that the Russians proposed. From the Yalta meeting in February on through the San Francisco Conference of the United Nations which did not wind up until the middle of June, the Polish question proved the major stumbling block to Big Three agreement and to the establishment of the United Nations Organization.

FISHING-POINT IN THE PACIFIC

ON February 19, 1945, United States Marines landed on Iwo Jima Island in the Volcano group, 750 miles from Tokyo. They fought for 26 days, losing more than 4,500 men killed and missing and more than 15,000 wounded. But they finally won a base from which medium bombers and long-range fighters could operate over Japan. The big B-29 superfortresses were already bombing Japan from the Mariannas Islands, making round trip flights of 3,000 miles. The possession of Iwo gave the superfortresses fighter protection and a base at which a number of the big disabled planes landed. And less than three weeks after enemy resistance had ended on Iwo, marines and soldiers were landing on Okinawa, only a little more than 300 miles from Japan.

Here with a Loaf of Bread beneath the Bough,
A Flask of Wine, a Book of Verse — and THOU
Beside us singing in the Wilderness—

THE RUBAIYAT: 1945 EDITION

AFTER the Yalta Conference, President Roosevelt stopped off in Cairo where he conferred on Middle Eastern matters with Prime Minister Churchill and with King Farouk of Egypt, Emperor Haile Selassie of Ethiopia, and King Ibn Saud of Saudi Arabia. He also suggested a conference with General De Gaulle at Algiers but De Gaulle turned him down. De Gaulle was still smarting from the succession of snubs he had received at the hands of all the Big Three leaders. Before D-Day, Roosevelt and Churchill had not let him in on all their plans. In December, 1944, he therefore signed a 20-year mutual assistance pact with the Russians whereupon Stalin proved even more obdurate than Roosevelt or Churchill and refused to consider inviting De Gaulle to Yalta. De Gaulle later retaliated by ordering French troops to crush native nationalists in Lebanon and Syria.

"TAXI, MISTER?"

ON March 7, 1945, one of those sudden breaks hastened—perhaps by months —the collapse of German resistance in the west. American infantrymen got over one of the bridges across the upper Rhine at Remagen before the Germans had a chance to blow it up. General Eisenhower suddenly decided to change all his plans and ordered an immediate exploitation of this unexpected advantage. Within a week, American troops had established a wide and secure bridgehead on the further bank of the Rhine. A breach had been made in Germany's last line of defense in the west.

"TAKE ME IN, MISTER?"

THE so-called Yalta formula whereby the Big Three had special voting and veto privileges in the projected United Nations security organization led to a good deal of criticism in Great Britain. Partly, it was a matter of principle. Partly, it was a matter of self-interest. Although David Low lampooned what he described as the "small nation mind" in connection with the demands of certain Poles for greater consideration, he—like many other people in Britain— believed that the Big Three had carried their domination a little too far at Yalta. Great Britain itself did not have the power of Russia or America. And the members of the British Commonwealth whose good will is essential to the mother country did not like the new set-up either.

KNELL

BY the middle of March, Hitler not only had a two front war on his hands.
Foreign Armies were invading Germany from the east and from the west, and
Allied air attacks had broken up German supply lines so completely that
Germany's military leaders were fighting two separate wars. Marshal Kesselring
who had directed a brilliant defensive campaign in Italy replaced Marshal
von Rundstedt as supreme commander in the west. And although the Russians
were fifty miles from Berlin, they were directing their main drive at Vienna
and the southern approaches to Germany.

"WELL, WELL, LOOK WHO'S HERE"

THE approach of the United Nations Conference at San Francisco, California, and the imminent collapse of Germany caused a last-minute rush for the victory bus. After the American Republics had met at Chapultepec in Mexico and voted to establish a system of regional security to be tied in with the United Nations' plans for world security, Argentina made a belated declaration of war on Germany and Japan and even Generalissimo Franco hinted that he might declare war on Japan if he—like Argentina—received an invitation to San Francisco. Although the Russians eventually accepted Argentina as a member of the United Nations (in exchange for the admission of three Soviet Republics to membership), the Soviet Union had never recognized Franco and his appeal for admission to San Francisco fell on deaf ears.

IRONING OUT THE CREASES

AS the opening date of the United Nations Conference at San Francisco drew near, the Polish question remained the principle obstacle in the way of Big Three agreement. The Russians had recognized as the provisional Polish government the group of Poles that had gradually rallied around the Union of Polish Patriots which had organized itself on Russian soil and under Russian auspices after the Russians broke with the Polish Exiled Government in 1943. Britain and the United States, on the other hand, continued to recognize the Polish Exiled government in London. Foreign Secretary Eden and Secretary of State Stettinius kept trying to bring these two rival groups of Poles together, without success. The London Poles refused to subordinate themselves to the pro-Russian faction. The pro-Russian Poles, for their part, insisted that their government must become the sole government of Poland— and the Russians backed this stand.

PROBABLY IT WILL GROW OUT OF IT (WE HOPE)

DURING the autumn of 1944 a series of conferences at Dumbarton Oaks, Virginia, among representatives of Britain, Russia, China, and the United States produced the first blue-print for the United Nations Organization. The Dumbarton Oaks Conference achieved agreement on all points but one. The Russians had insisted that the major powers with permanent seats on the projected security council could veto any action against themselves. The Yalta Conference came up with a compromise arrangement which only gradually saw the light of day. The so-called Yalta formula gave the smaller nations more than the Russians had been willing to grant at Dumbarton Oaks, but not enough to satisfy the foreign ministers of the British Dominions or other representatives of the so-called middle and smaller powers.

LAST TRIBUTE

THE British have seldom mourned the death of any of their own leaders as they mourned the death of President Roosevelt on April 13, 1945. The man in the street compared it to the passing of George V and of Queen Victoria. Prime Minister Churchill wept as he paid tribute to Mr. Roosevelt on the floor of the House of Commons. It was not only what President Roosevelt had done to help the British in their darkest hours and to bring America into the war. It was the feeling that President Roosevelt died even before his greatest work had begun. Allied armies had all but won the victory. The great task of winning the peace remained.

HAND-CLASPS

GENERAL Eisenhower deliberately ordered the Allied armies advancing into Germany from the west to halt on the banks of the River Elbe, less than 100 miles from Berlin. He not only respected the decision of the Yalta Conference to give the Red Army the honor of occupying the German capital; Allied troops had already advanced beyond the previously agreed occupation zones and the Elbe River provided a natural stopping-point. But Allied and Russian troops did join up before the Russians had taken Berlin. Some of them met at the southern end of the front, in Czechoslovakia. Others met on the banks of the Elbe to which some Russians had advanced before they took the by-passed German capital.

GERMAN GUILT

AS the Russian armies moved into Germany from the east and as Allied armies moved into Germany from the west, they came upon a succession of horror camps—Dachau, Buchenwald, and Belsen. The revelations of the atrocities that the Germans had committed in these camps led at first to incredulity and then to a demand to punish the whole German people. But men like David Low who had depicted the horror of these camps for years recalled that the Nazis had originally set them up for the purpose of torturing and killing their own people. A few anti-Nazi Germans had survived not only the war but the pre-war years and some people hoped that from their ranks might be recruited the leaders of a new Germany. But most of those who had survived were broken in health and spirit.

THE ACCURSED CITY

ON April 20, 1945, Russian troops entered Berlin and the final, desperate battle of the eastern front was on. Marshal Zhukov who organized the attack on Berlin had some two million men under his command, but he had released no news since the key city of Kuestrin, fifty miles east of Berlin, had fallen on March 18. After ordering minor offensives both to the north and the south of Berlin, Zhukov ordered a massive artillery barrage—the favorite Russian offensive weapon. Four thousand tanks and five thousand planes also went into action, for the Germans had prepared strong defenses. But these defenses held for only two days. For the Red Army, the supreme moment of the war had come.

"AFTER YOU—"

ON April 25, 1945, representatives of the forty-six United Nations met at San Francisco to organize a system of world security. It afforded several contrasts with the League of Nations. The League had not been organized until the First World War had ended. It was tied in with the peace treaties. It did not require its members to use force against aggression. The United Nations on the other hand met while the war was still in progress. They planned to rely on power to enforce law. The victorious powers after the First World War had written the major treaties and drawn up the League Covenant within six months' time. The victorious powers after the Second World War moved much more slowly.

TAILPIECE TO GLORY

ON April 28, Mussolini died as violently and ingloriously as he had lived. His own countrymen executed him and his mistress and sixteen fellow-Fascists in the north Italian village of Dongo on Lake Como. Not satisfied with having made an end of the former Duce, his executioners carried the dead bodies to Milan where crowds spat on them and kicked them about the streets. At last they were buried, unmarked, in potter's field. As the trials of other war criminals ran their dreary course in later months, some people wished that all of them had suffered the crude justice meted out to Mussolini, by his own people. But would the Germans have turned as violently against Hitler?

LAST SHOT FOR "THE HITLER LEGEND"

ON May 1, 1945, three days after Mussolini met his death, the German radio at Hamburg announced that Hitler died fighting in the streets of Berlin. Subsequent investigation indicated that Hitler, like Mussolini, had died with his mistress but that he had made an honest woman of her in a marriage ceremony just before the end. In any event Hitler and Eva Braun spent their last days in the cellars of the Reichschancellory and when Hitler saw his cause was hopeless, both of them decided to shoot themselves and left instructions that their bodies should be burned to prevent their falling into Russian hands. There is also strong reason to believe that Hitler had suffered a complete mental and physical breakdown before he finally took his own life.

END? NO, BEGINNING

BEFORE the Russians took Berlin their soldiers had established contact with the British and Americans at many points. Things went uncommonly well among them all. The British and Americans had already overcome many of their prejudices as they fought their way from the Normandy beaches to the banks of the Elbe. And the Russians were so gratified with the results of the Second Front that they welcomed their Anglo-American allies as comrades in arms. Never since the Russian Revolution did the common man in the Soviet Union feel so well-disposed toward the people of the west.

THE NIGHTMARE PASSES

VE DAY came in three instalments. On May 7, 1945, Edward Kennedy of the Associated Press released the premature announcement that General Eisenhower had accepted the unconditional surrender of the German Armies from General Jodl, chief of staff of the German Army, the day before. On May 8, President Truman and King George officially announced Germany's unconditional surrender to the American and British people. The Russians postponed their celebrations until May 9 when Marshal Zhukov received the surrender of Field Marshal Keitel, commander in chief of the German armies, in Berlin.

"A FINE TEAM—BUT COULD DO WITH A DASH OF UNITY..."

ON June 5, 1945, the commanders of the American, British, French, and Russian armies in Germany issued a four-power declaration in Berlin proclaiming the complete defeat of Germany. On June 26, representatives of fifty United Nations signed the world security charter at San Francisco. Not only were a few major powers tending to dominate the United Nations. Each of these great powers reserved to itself its own national sovereignty. Thus, the five permanent members of the United Nations Security Council dominated the organization. At the same time, each of these five powers had the right to veto any action that the United Nations might take.

DAY AFTER

ON July 5, 1945, the British people elected their first new House of Commons in ten years. The results of the voting were not made known until July 26 when the Big Three Conference at Potsdam had already spent ten days wrestling with post-war problems. To the amazement of the whole world, the British Labor Party gained an overwhelming majority of seats in the new Parliament. Clement Attlee who had taken part in all the Potsdam conversations organized a new Cabinet and flew back to Potsdam with his new Foreign Secretary, Ernest Bevin. The Conservatives had tried to convince the electorate that Harold Laski, the Secretary of the Labor Party, was plotting to install Communism in the British Isles, but Mr. Laski's progressive ideas did not get much of a chance. When Mr. Laski asked Mr. Bevin if he could do anything to help the new government, Bevin is reported to have replied, "Yes. Keep quiet."

"COMPLETE SURRENDER—INCLUDING FACE"

ON the same day that the British election results became known, the American, British, and Chinese governments issued the so-called Potsdam Declaration calling for the unconditional surrender of Japan. The Japanese at once rejected the proposals. On August 6, American planes dropped the first atomic bomb on Hiroshima. Two days later, the Russians declared war on Japan and endorsed the Potsdam terms. In another two days the Japanese sued for peace but asked to be permitted to retain their Emperor. The Allies replied that the Emperor must take orders from the victorious powers—and the Japanese accepted. They had lost everything—including face.

"THIRD ACT — CURTAIN"

THE final act of the Second World War took place on the deck of the U.S.S. *Missouri* in Tokyo Bay where General MacArthur and the military leaders of the other Allied powers received the formal surrender of the Japanese government. The war had cost a toll of death and ruin beyond all calculation. Most of the fighting had taken place in Asia and Europe and on the Atlantic and Pacific Oceans. But men from every continent had lost their lives in the struggle and the resources of every continent had been drained.

THE WRECKED WORLD

"—AND NOW TO WORK"

WINNING the peace presented as great a challenge as winning the war. The Soviet Union had sustained the greatest physical damage of any of the major belligerents. The Chinese had suffered the greatest losses of life. The people of Western Europe had suffered the greatest loss of power. For the first time in five hundred years, the center of world power no longer lay in Europe but had shifted to Russia and the United States. To rebuild the wreckage of war required a tremendous physical, material effort. But a political and moral effort was needed too, a determination on the part of all peoples to work together.

1931

September 19. Japanese troops seize strategic points in Manchuria.

20. Great Britain abandons gold standard.

October 9. Secretary of State Stimson informs Geneva that the United States will try to help League of Nations end warfare between Japanese and Chinese forces in Manchuria.

13. Japanese planes bomb Chinese troops while League of Nations discusses Manchurian crisis.

18. Japanese Government rejects League of Nations proposals for settling Manchurian dispute and criticizes United States policy.

20. United States Government reminds Japan and China of their obligations under Kellogg-Briand Pact outlawing war as instrument of national policy.

24. Council of League of Nations calls upon Japan to evacuate Manchuria by November 16.

27. British National Government wins 553 seats in the House of Commons at general election following abandonment of gold standard. Labor opposition wins 59 seats.

December 9. Spanish Parliament adopts a new Republican Constitution.

11. Japan's Liberal Minseito Cabinet resigns. New elections ordered.

28. Chinese Central Government at Nanking reorganizes, as progressives oust Chiang Kai-shek and Finance Minister, T. V. Soong.

1932

January 2. British authorities arrest Mahatma Gandhi on eve of civil disobedience campaign to which he had summoned all of India. His All-India Congress Party also outlawed.

7. Secretary of State Stimson sends identic note to Japan and China invoking the Nine-Power Pact that upheld the territorial integrity of China. British Foreign Secretary Sir John Simon refuses to follow Stimson's lead.

9. Prime Minister Pierre Laval reshuffles the French Cabinet, taking over Ministry of Foreign Affairs from Aristide Briand.

23. Moratorium on German short-term credits owed to foreign countries extended another year.

25. Chiang Kai-shek resumes control of Chinese National Government.

28. Japanese forces open attack on Chapei, Chinese native quarter of Shanghai.

February 1. Japanese troops land at Nanking as Chapei bombardment continues.

2. Disarmament Conference opens at Geneva. America, Britain, France, and Italy make joint proposals to settle Chinese-Japanese war.

4. Japan refuses request of Western Powers to cease hostilities and rejects arbitration proposals. Russia protests Japanese use of Chinese Eastern Railway.

9. Former Finance Minister Inouye of Japan assassinated in Tokyo.

18. Manchuria and Inner Mongolia proclaim their independence from China

and establish puppet government subordinate to Japan.

20. The Conservative Seiyukai Party wins control of Japanese Parliament from the Liberal Minseito Party, 304 seats to 147.

March 2. Japanese break Chinese defenses and occupy Chapei.

9. Japanese install Henry Pu-yi as puppet emperor of Manchuria—renamed Manchukuo.

April 10. Von Hindenburg re-elected President of Germany by 2,235,000 majority.

24. Nazis win more seats than any other party in Prussian Parliament, but not outright majority.

May 5. Japanese and Chinese representatives sign agreement at Shanghai whereby Japanese withdraw troops and Chinese cease boycott of Japanese goods.

6. President Doumer of France assassinated by White Russian.

8. French Radical Socialist Party led by Edouard Herriot wins control of Chamber of Deputies.

10. Albert Lebrun, independent conservative, elected President of French Republic.

15. Members of secret society of militarists assassinate Prime Minister Inukai of Japan.

22. Admiral Saito, independent conservative, succeeds Inukai as Japanese Prime Minister.

30. Heinrich Bruening, leader of Catholic Center Party, resigns as Chancellor of Germany. Franz von Papen sets up a Nationalist government based on a Reichstag minority to replace the Bruening coalition government which had rested on a Reichstag majority.

June 3. Edouard Herriot forms a Radical Socialist government in France, replacing Tardieu's nationalist-conservative regime.

4. President von Hindenburg dissolves the German Reichstag and calls for new elections. The von Papen cabinet continues to govern by decree.

16. Republican National Convention unanimously renominates President Hoover and Vice President Curtis.

22. President Hoover communicates immediate disarmament plan to Geneva.

July 1. Democratic National Convention nominates Roosevelt-Garner ticket to oppose Hoover and Curtis.

8. Lausanne Reparations Conference agrees to free Germany of all further reparations payments in consideration of small lump sum payment and with provision that United States scale down war debts again.

20. President von Hindenburg issues emergency decree ousting Social Democratic administration of Prussia.

21. British Imperial Conference opens at Ottawa.

31. German National Socialists win more Reichstag seats than any other party but fall short of majority.

August 20. British Imperial Conference at Ottawa ends after signing twelve trade agreements strengthening empire trade and raising tariff barriers for five-year period.

31. New German Reichstag elects Hermann Goering president.

September 12. New German Reichstag votes non-confidence in von Papen government, 513 to 32, but von Papen dissolves Reichstag again and continues to govern by decree since no leader can win a majority.

15. Japanese government and puppet government of Manchukuo sign defensive agreement in which Japan recognizes Manchukuo as an independent state.

28. Viscount Snowden, Laborite, and Sir Herbert Samuel and Sir Archibald Sinclair, Liberals, resign from Ramsay MacDonald's British National Government and join opposition.

October 2. The Lytton Commission, appointed by League of Nations to investigate Manchurian situation at first hand, files its report finding Japan guilty of aggression and treaty-breaking.

November 6. National Socialist vote in German Reichstag election shows two million decrease. Communists, with more than six million votes, score largest gain. Nationalists and People's Parties show slight gain; Social Democrats slight loss.

8. Franklin D. Roosevelt elected President of the United States. Democrats win control of both Houses of Congress.

17. Von Papen Cabinet resigns in Germany.

20. Japanese file reply to Lytton Report with League of Nations.

29. France and Soviet Union sign non-aggression pact.

December 3. General von Schleicher forms new German Cabinet, bringing in more parties than von Papen.

14. Herriot Government in France falls as Chamber of Deputies votes to defer war debt payments to the United States.

20. Von Schleicher Cabinet restores freedom of press and assembly in Germany.

1933

January 1. Soviet Union announces completion of First Five Year Plan in four years. Heavy stress on industrialization leads to food shortages and famine.

11. Japanese troops gain control of all highways leading from Manchuria to Jehol-Province in North China.

17. United States Senate passes bill approving independence for Philippine Islands over President Hoover's veto.

27. Chancellor von Schleicher resigns in Germany.

30. President von Hindenburg appoints Adolf Hitler German Chancellor as head of coalition government of Nazis and Nationalists.

February 17. League of Nations unanimously denounces Japanese occupation of Manchuria as incompatible with Kellogg Pact outlawing war, with Nine Power Treaty underwriting China's integrity, and with League Covenant.

27. German Reichstag building destroyed by fire set by Nazis.

28. Hitler issues emergency decree suspending constitutional guarantees in Germany.

March 4. Franklin D. Roosevelt inaugurated President of the United States.

5. National Socialists and Nationalists win majority of seats in German Reichstag elections. Japanese troops enter Jehol City.

9. Congress of the United States meeting in emergency session called by President Roosevent, votes President dictatorial control over credit, currency, and foreign exchange.

23. German Reichstag confers blanket powers to Hitler Government for four year period.

April 1. Nazis order one-day boycott of Jewish shops in Germany.

12. Pope Pius XI receives Vice Chancellor von Papen of Germany and Prime Minister Goering of Prussia in private audience.

19. King George V proclaims British embargo on Russian goods two days after expiration of Anglo-Soviet trade agreement.

May 16. President Roosevelt invites 54 nations to begin reducing armaments and sign a general non-aggression agreement.

17. Hitler accepts Roosevelt proposals on condition that all nations have proportionate equality of armament.

31. Japanese and Chinese sign truce establishing neutral zone south of Great Wall.

June 4. Reconstruction Finance Corporation extends $50,000,000 credit to Chinese National Government for purchase of American cotton and wheat.

12. World Economic Conference opens at London.

19. Austrian Government outlaws Nazis.

22. German Government outlaws Socialists and removes all Socialists from public office.

23. Recently neutralized North China area declares its independence through a group of war lords.

29. German Nationalist Party dissolves and joins the Nazi Party.

July 3. President Roosevelt informs World Economic Conference that United States cannot return to gold standard.

4. Catholic Center Party and other smaller moderate parties in Germany disband.

20. Germany and the Vatican sign a concordat.

27. World Economic Conference adjourns.

August 3. United States Navy Department awards contracts on record naval building program.

September 20. Chancellor Dollfuss of Austria forms a Catholic Fascist Government.

October 3. President Roosevelt invites Russian delegation to discuss establishment of Russian-American diplomatic relations.

14. German Government withdraws from the League of Nations.

November 12. Ninety-two per cent of German electorate approve Hitler's resignation from the League and withdrawal from the Disarmament Conference.

16. United States and Soviet Union open diplomatic relations.

20. Chinese Province of Fukien declares itself an independent Republic.

December 8. Anarchist uprisings throughout Spain.

January 23. Admirals of British, Australian, and New Zealand fleets confer at Singapore.

26. Germany and Poland sign ten-year peace pact.

February 6. Seventeen killed and 500 injured in Paris riots.

7. Newly formed leftist cabinet of Premier Daladier resigns and ex-President Doumergue emerges from retirement to head national coalition government.

12. General strikes paralyze France and Austria. Dollfuss orders Austrian troops to attack workers' quarter in Vienna, killing more than 100 people.

15. French Chamber of Deputies gives Doumergue Cabinet heavy vote of confidence and Austrian Socialists yield as their leaders flee abroad.

March 1. Henry Pu-yi, hereditary Manchu Emperor of China, ascends throne of puppet state of Manchukuo and assumes title of Kang Teh.

April 18. Japanese Foreign Office spokesman announces Japan "may be compelled to resort to force" to maintain peace in Asia.

23. British Foreign Office challenges Japan's claim to special rights in China.

28. Japanese assure Britain and the United States that they have "no wish to infringe on the independence, interests, or prosperity of China."

30. United States warns Japan to respect treaties in China. Britain considers issue with Japan over China closed.

May 7. British impose quotas on textile imports from Japan.

June 14. Germany declares moratorium on all foreign debts.

15. Hitler and Mussolini meet for the first time and pledge support to Austrian independence after conferring in Venice.

30. Former Chancellor von Schleicher and several hundred Storm Troop leaders die in Nazi blood purge.

July 9. Hitler orders Storm Troops disarmed and their ranks reduced from over 2 million to 850,000.

15. French Socialists vote to form united front with Communists.

16. Japanese Ambassador to London halts naval talks with Anglo-Americans.

25. Austrian Nazis assassinate Chancellor Dollfuss of Austria but fail to seize power.

26. Vice Chancellor von Papen named German Ambassador to Austria as Italy sends 48,000 additional troops to Austrian border with approval of France.

29. Kurt Schuschnigg, Austrian monarchist, heads new Austrian government.

30. Yugoslav Legation in Berlin cautions Italy not to intervene in Austria.

August 2. President von Hindenburg of Germany dies. Hitler assumes all his powers, appoints Dr. Schacht Minister of Economics, and orders plebiscite.

19. German plebiscite approves granting Hitler supreme power as Reichsfuehrer, giving him 90 percent of all votes cast.

September 10. Germany rejects "East European Locarno Pact" that would guarantee status quo in Eastern Europe.

18. Soviet Russia joins the League of Nations.

October 5. All Spain placed under martial law as Socialist and Communist leaders call general strike in protest against addition of three Catholic Popular Actionists to Cabinet.

9. Croatian terrorists with Italian and Hungarian connivance assassinate King Alexander I of Yugoslavia in streets of Marseilles. Foreign Minister Barthou of France also killed as he returns from swing through Russia and Balkans where he had made new security treaties.

16. Spanish government troops kill 600 rebels in Asturias as revolts continue.

November 5. Japanese Foreign Office informs Britain and the United States that projected government oil monopoly in puppet state of Manchukuo does not violate Open Door policy.

7. Premier Lerroux of Spain extends martial law another 30 days.

12. Chinese government troops capture Communist capital of Juichin in Kiangsi Province.

15. Spanish Cortes votes to disqualify all deputies involved in revolts.

22. Yugoslav, Czechoslovak, and Rumanian governments, representing the pro-French Little Entente, protest to League of Nations that Hungary endangers peace in Central Europe.

23. French Chamber of Deputies learns that Russia has offered to enter an alliance with France to fight Germany in the event of German attack.

December 1. Sergei Mironovich Kirov, close friend of Stalin and one of ten-man Politbureau that heads Soviet State, assassinated in Leningrad.

10. League of Nations Council unanimously approves settlement of Yugoslav-Hungarian dispute whereby Hungary agrees to take action against any citizens implicated in murder of King Alexander.

16. Zinoviev, Kamenev, and thirteen other Old Bolsheviks arrested by Soviet government.

29. Japanese government formally denounces Washington Naval Limitation Treaty of 1922, effective January 1, 1937.

1935

January 3. Ethiopia asks League of Nations to take effective action to safeguard peace between itself and Italy.

13. More than 90 per cent of the inhabitants of the Saar Valley vote under League plebiscite and terms of Versailles Treaty to return from French rule to German.

15. Zinoviev, Kamenev, and 17 other Old Bolsheviks go on trial as counter-revolutionaries.

29. Several Italian and Ethiopian soldiers killed in border patrol clash. Italy demands apologies, indemnities, and frontier changes.

March 16. German Government re-establishes military conscription.

18. British Government protests German conscription.

21. German government rejects foreign protests against conscription.

23. Italian Government summons Class of 1911 to the colors and plans to have 600,000 men under arms by August.

25. Hitler receives British Foreign Secretary Simon and Anthony Eden in Berlin

after discussion of European security. Hitler announces German Air Force now equals Britain's.

28. Anthony Eden confers with Foreign Commissar Litvinov and then meets Stalin in Moscow to discuss European security.

April 7. Nazi Party wins majority of seats in the council of the Free City of Danzig.

11. British, French and Italian governments open Three-Power security talks at Stresa and agree to work through League and to oppose unilateral treaty violations.

13. German government agrees to support Stresa decisions with reservations.

16. British, French, and Italian governments agree on resolution to be laid before League of Nations condemning German treaty violations and providing for action in case of future difficulties.

17. Prime Minister MacDonald announces Stresa decisions do not involve any new British commitments in Europe and leave door open for inclusion of Germany in future negotiation.

18. German government protests British "betrayal" of Germany at Stresa and Geneva.

May 21. Hitler announces that Germany has repudiated only armament restrictions in Versailles Treaty and will respect all others, but seek readjustments.

22. British House of Commons votes 340 to 53 to triple expenditures on Royal Air Force in order to keep up with German air armaments.

June 6. Pierre Laval forms new French government in which he holds posts of Premier and Foreign Minister.

July 17. Emperor Haile Selassie offers Ethiopian territory to Italy in exchange for a Red Sea port.

August 28. Mussolini warns foreign powers not to attempt to apply sanctions to Italy

September 6. League of Nations appoints five-power conciliation council to investigate Italian-Ethiopian dispute. Ethiopia agrees to cooperate. Italy refuses.

9. British Foreign Secretary Sir Samuel Hoare and French Premier Laval pledge themselves and their countries to observe all League of Nations obligations, as 16th meeting of League Council opens.

10. Mussolini orders mobilization of 10,000,000 Italians and calls 50,000 more men to the colors.

12. Secretary of State Hull reminds Italy and Ethiopia of their obligations under Kellogg Pact to outlaw war as an instrument of national policy and settle all disputes peacefully.

14. Italian Government announces that it cannot accept any compromise solution of Ethiopian dispute.

15. German Reichstag meets in Nazi shrine city of Nurenberg; adopts swastika as Germany's national flag; passes extensive anti-Semitic laws.

18. League of Nations offers plan for international assistance to Ethiopia with Italy's special interests recognized. Ethiopia accepts; Italy gives qualified refusal.

25. President Roosevelt proclaims list of war munitions that must be registered under Neutrality Act.

28. Italy rejects League proposal to settle dispute with Ethiopia.

October 2. Ethiopian government declares Italian troops violate Ethiopian frontier.

3. Italians admit their troops have begun to march into Ethiopia but accuse Ethiopians of firing at their planes.

5. President Roosevelt embargoes arms shipments to Italy or Ethiopia under terms of Neutrality Act. Ethiopia invokes League sanctions—the first time one League member has accused another of aggression.

6. Italian troops capture Adowa.

10. League Assembly votes 51 to 3 that Italy has violated Covenant by attacking Ethiopia.

16. British government rejects plea of French Premier Laval to ithdraw any of 150 British war vessels from the Mediterranean.

19. League of Nations votes to apply sanctions against Italy—Hungary and Albania abstaining. Prime Minister Baldwin denies that Britain plans to overthrow Italian Fascism.

22. Foreign Secretary Hoare announces that Britain will not close Suez Canal to Italian ships or impose military sanctions against Italy.

30. President Roosevelt and Secretary Hull suggest stopping all American trade with Italy as means to end war.

November 14. Conservative Party wins majority of 244 seats in House of Commons, giving Baldwin government five more years in office.

16. Marshal Badoglio appointed to replace General de Bono to direct Italian campaign in Ethiopia.

December 18. Sir Samuel Hoare resigns as British Foreign Secretary following revelation that he and Premier Laval had agreed to dismember Ethiopia to benefit of Italy.

19. House of Commons votes confidence in Baldwin government which admits error in having approved Hoare-Laval Pact.

1936

January 20. King George V of England dies and is succeeded by Edward VIII.

February 16. Leftist Parties win majority of seats in Spanish parliamentary elections.

18. Spanish government arrests many Conservative leaders for plotting armed insurrection. Other Conservatives quit Spain.

19. Former Premier Azaña organizes new Spanish Republican government.

25. Several thousand Japanese troops in Tokyo garrison assassinate leading Cabinet members following victory of anti-militarist parties in parliamentary elections. Prime Minister Okada escapes death but rebels hold part of Tokyo.

29. Japanese rebels surrender to government forces.

March 4. Soviet government reveals it will go to war rather than permit Japanese encroachment in Mongolian People's Republic.

5. League of Nations publishes telegram from Emperor Haile Selassie accept-

ing its mediation offer provided Italians accept League Covenant.

7. German troops violate Versailles Treaty and Locarno Pact by marching into demilitarized Rhineland cities. Hitler justifies action on ground that Franco-Soviet mutual assistance pact frees Germany from Locarno agreement not to remilitarize the Rhineland. France and other signatories of Locarno Pact protest to League of Nations.

9. Koki Hirota, former Japanese Foreign Minister, organizes new conservative government.

19. League of Nations Council votes unanimously that German remilitarization of Rhineland violates Locarno Treaty.

25. Britain, France, and the United States sign naval limitation treaty.

29. German plebiscite gives Hitler policies 98.79% support.

April 1. Germany agrees not to increase armed forces in Rhineland during next four months if France and Belgium send no additional troops to their side of the border.

20. League of Nations names Italy the aggressor in Ethiopian war, urges continuation of sanctions, and again proposes peace.

29. Germans and Russians extend long-standing trade agreement.

May 2. Emperor Haile Selassie and family quit capital city of Addis Ababa.

3. Popular Front parties in France—Socialists, Radicals, and Communists—win majority of seats in Chamber of Deputies elections.

5. Marshal Badoglio's troops reach Addis Ababa.

9. Mussolini announces formal annexation of Ethiopia by Italy and King Victor Emmanuel assumes title of Emperor.

10. Spanish electoral college chooses Manuel Azaña as Spanish president.

11. Council of League of Nations rejects Italian demand to drop Ethiopian question and continues to recognize Ethiopian delegation. Italian delegation walks out.

June 4. French Socialist government headed by Léon Blum and supported by Popular Front coalition takes office. Sit-down strikers win demands for higher pay and shorter hours.

23. British House of Commons votes 384 to 170 to drop sanctions against Italy.

30. Emperor Haile Selassie appeals to League of Nations Assembly for aid.

July 15. League of Nations' sanctions against Italy ended.

19. Spanish rebels start uprising against Republic as foreign legion troops land from Spanish Morocco at Cadiz and Spanish garrisons seize several cities.

25. Spanish army chiefs set up provisional government in northern cities as General Franco crosses from Morocco to lead drive from south.

August 23. Moscow court sentences sixteen oppositionists, including Old Bolsheviks Zinoviev, Kamenev, and Smirnov to death for plotting to kill Stalin.

24. German government announces embargo on arms shipments to Spain, following similar action by Britain, France, and Russia.

October 14. Belgian government severs all military alliances and reverts to pre-war policy of neutrality in case of war.

29. Spanish Loyalists with new equipment repel rebel thrust into University City of Madrid after several months of increasingly bitter fighting marked by many rebel gains.

November 3. Roosevelt-Garner ticket wins American Presidential election, carrying all States except Maine and Vermont.

28. Russians back Spanish plea to League of Nations to restrain German and Italian aid to Franco, but British and French oppose Russian stand.

December 1. President Roosevelt tells Inter-American Conference for the Maintenance of Peace at Buenos Aires that New World nations should unite to help Europe avert war and should stand together against any outside aggression.

11. British Parliament ratifies abdication of King Edward VIII.

14. King George VI of England delivers first message to Parliament.

15. President Roosevelt returns from South American cruise.

16. The Inter-American Conference for the Maintenance of Peace unanimously adopts collective security convention and nonintervention protocol.

1937

January 2. Britain and Italy sign Mediterranean agreement.

8. President Roosevelt signs Congressional resolution embargoing arms shipments to Spain.

23. Moscow trial of Karl Radek and others begins.

30. Hitler announces that Germany repudiates war-guilt clause in Versailles Treaty.

February 8. City of Malaga in Mediterranean surrenders to General Franco.

March 5. Central Executive Committee of Russian Communist Party announces introduction of secret ballot and expulsion of Rykov and Bukharin.

25. British government accedes to request of France and releases Belgium from obligations of material assistance under the Locarno Pact.

April 19. British, French, German, and Italian warships begin patroling Spanish coast under Nonintervention Agreement.

May 1. President Roosevelt signs Neutrality Act.

12. George VI crowned King and Emperor.

17. Juan Negrin forms new Republican government in Loyalist Spain following failure of Largo Caballero to work with Communists.

28. Neville Chamberlain succeeds Stanley Baldwin as British Prime Minister.

29. Spanish Loyalists bomb German cruiser *Deutschland* off the Balearic Islands.

31. German war vessels bombard Spanish port of Almeria in retaliation for *Deutschland* shelling.

June 11. Marshal Tukhatchevsky and seven other Russian generals sentenced to be shot for treason.

19. Franco's troops occupy Bilbao, Basque seaport in northern Spain.

20. Popular Front government of Premier Léon Blum resigns in France.

22. Camille Chautemps forms new French government with Blum as Vice-Premier.

23. Germany and Italy withdraw from Four-Power naval patrol of Spanish coast.

29. French government suspends gold and foreign-exchange payments.

July 2. Soviet government withdraws patrols and naval cutters from Amur River islands for which Japan disputes ownership.

17. England signs naval limitation treaties with Germany and Russia.

27. German government requisitions all wheat and rye crops.

29. Japanese bombing planes attack Tientsin in first major attack of Japanese undeclared war on China.

August 9. Japanese troops enter ancient Chinese capital of Peiping.

25. President Roosevelt signs modified Supreme Court Procedure Act.

26. Japanese machine gunners from low-flying airplane wound British Ambassador to China.

28. Secretary Hull notifies Japan and China that the United States reserves all rights on its own behalf and on that of its nationals in connection with wartime damages.

29. Chinese government signs nonaggression pact with the Soviet Union.

September 6. Soviet government accuses Italian vessels of sinking two Russian vessels bound for Spain.

7. Hitler tells Nuremberg Nazi Congress that Germany, Italy, and Japan are linked to save Europe from "chaotic madness."

10. Britain, France, Russia, and six smaller Mediterranean nations announce that submarines will operate in the Mediterranean at their own risk. Germany, Italy, and Albania refuse to attend meeting at Nyon, on the Swiss border of France, from which the statement came.

14. President Roosevelt announces that merchant vessels owned by the United States will be permitted to carry arms and munitions to China and Japan.

25. Mussolini visits Hitler at Munich and reviews army maneuvers in Berlin the next day.

28. Mussolini proclaims solidarity of Rome-Berlin Axis in broadcast address at Berlin.

October 5. President Roosevelt calls for a "quarantine" of "aggressor nations" in Chicago speech.

6. United States State Department condemns Japan for violating Nine-Power Treaty and Briand-Kellogg anti-war pact.

9. Italy refuses Anglo-French invitation to discuss withdrawal of troops from Spain.

13. Germany pledges to respect Belgian neutrality under all circumstances.

29. Germany declines Belgian invitation to Nine-Power Conference at Brussels to discuss the war in China.

November 6. Italy joins Germany and Japan in Anti-Comintern Pact.

28. Spanish Rebel government proclaims blockade of all Loyalist ports.

29. Italy recognizes independence of Manchukuo.

December 12. Japanese bombing planes sink U. S. gunboat *Panay* on the Yangtze River.

14. Japan establishes new puppet Chinese government at Nanking.

24. Japan assures the United States in reply to *Panay* protest that American rights will be respected. The next day the State Department calls the reply satisfactory.

1938

January 12. First session of new Red Parliament opens in Moscow.

February 12. Chancellor Schuschnigg of Austria confers with Hitler at Berchtesgaden and consents to take five Nazi sympathizers into his cabinet.

21. Foreign Minister Anthony Eden resigns from the Chamberlain Cabinet because of the Prime Minister's insistence on concluding a pact with Mussolini, notwithstanding Italy's violation of the Nonintervention Agreement in Spain.

March 9. Chancellor Schuschnigg of Austria announces that a plebiscite will be held on March 13 to determine whether the Austrian people prefer to maintain their independence or join Germany.

11. Chancellor Schuschnigg resigns as Austrian Premier to forestall immediate German armed intervention. The new Premier, Seyss-Inquart, calls for German troops and on March 13 proclaims the union of Germany and Austria.

April 16. Britain and Italy sign a peace and harmony pact, contingent upon the withdrawal of Italian forces from Spain.

24. Konrad Henlein, leader of the Nazis in Sudetenland, reveals his eight-point "Karlsbad Program" of demands to be made upon the Czechoslovak government.

May 20. Czechoslovak forces mobilize in response to German mobilization on Czechoslovakian frontier.

July 2. The Czechoslovak government rejects several of the eight Karlsbad demands laid before it by the Sudeten Nazis.

August 3. Lord Runciman arrives in Prague as Britain's "conciliator and mediator" of the Czechoslovak crisis.

15. German army maneuvers of unprecedented size begin and continue for a full month.

22. The Soviet Union informs the German ambassador at Moscow that Russia will stand by its 1935 promise to support Czechoslovakia in the event of attack.

September 12. Hitler tells Nuremberg Congress that Czech oppression of Sudeten Germans must end.

15. Chamberlain flies to Berchtesgaden to confer with Hitler.

18. Premier Daladier and Foreign Minister Bonnet of France confer with the British in London and agree upon dismemberment of Czechoslovakia.

22. The Czechoslovak government accepts Anglo-French terms calling for virtual surrender to Germany.

24. Chamberlain brings back from his Godesberg meeting with Hitler the day before a new list of German demands on Czechoslovakia, far exceeding

those the British and French had urged the Czechs to make. Czechoslovakia mobilizes.

29. Mussolini, Hitler, Daladier, and Chamberlain meet at Munich and agree on terms calling for partitioning of Czechoslovakia.

30. The Czechoslovak government accepts the terms of the Munich Conference.

October 10. German troops and Gestapo agents complete the occupation of the ceded areas of Czechoslovakia, sometimes going beyond the boundaries agreed upon at Munich.

November 7. Herschel Grynzspan, 17-year old Polish Jew, in a fit of manic depression, shoots Ernst vom Rath of the German embassy in Paris, following expulsion of all Polish Jews from the Reich.

13. Goering announces that German Jews must pay for damages done them by German mobs following the shooting of vom Rath, plus a fine of one billion marks for the death of vom Rath. This leads President Roosevelt to summon American Ambassador Hugh Wilson to return to Washington to report. The Germans also recall their envoy from Washington.

1939

January 25. General Franco's troops take Barcelona.

February 2. The Soviet Union severs diplomatic relations with Hungary because that country recently signed the Anti-Comintern Pact.

7. Over a million Spanish refugees enter France as Loyalist troops continue retreats.

28. Chamberlain announces that Great Britain will recognize the Franco regime as the legal Spanish government.

March 10. Stalin delivers speech to 18th Party Congress of the Soviet Union criticizing appeasement and warning that Russia will not pull other nations' chestnuts out of the fire.

13. Hitler summons President Hacha, successor to Eduard Benes as President of Czechoslovakia, to Berlin. Father Tiso declares Slovakia a separate state.

15. Hitler extends his protection to Czechoslovakia, extinguishing the republic, as German troops enter Prague.

20. Rumania signs a trade treaty with Germany.

21. Lithuania surrenders the city of Memel to Germany.

29. The remains of Republican Spain surrender to General Franco.

31. Great Britain guarantees Poland against aggression.

April 7. Italian troops invade Albania and five days later King Victor Emmanuel II accepts the Albanian crown.

15. Roosevelt asks Hitler and Mussolini to pledge ten years of peace and lists 27 countries that they should promise not to attack.

28. Hitler rejects Roosevelt's peace proposal and denounces the Anglo-German naval treaty and his own nonaggression pact with Poland.

May 5. Foreign Commissar Maxim Litvinov, leading Soviet exponent of collective security, resigns his post and is replaced by Vyacheslav Molotov.

10. Prime Minister Chamberlain makes his first statement on his secret and unsuccessful efforts to secure Russian collaboration.

June 7. William Strang of the British Foreign Office goes to Moscow to try to work out some Anglo-Russian agreement.

22. King George and Queen Elizabeth return from their visit to Canada and the United States.

August 13. Climaxing months of agitation and infiltration of Germans into the Free City of Danzig, Hitler invites Dr. Burckhardt, League of Nations Commissioner, to a conference at Berchtesgaden.

22. German Foreign Minister von Ribbentrop flies to Moscow to sign a ten-year nonaggression pact with the Soviet Union.

25. The British and Poles sign a mutual-assistance pact in London.

27. Hitler refuses Daladier's appeal to make one more attempt to negotiate with Poland, insisting that Danzig and the Polish Corridor must return to the Reich.

28. France closes the German frontier.

30. Hitler rejects British appeal that he negotiate with Poland but does not show the Poles the terms that the British Ambassador in Berlin is told were offered to them.

September 1. German troops invade Poland without formal declaration of war. The British and French ambassadors in Berlin announce that unless German troops are withdrawn immediately, their respective countries will fulfill their obligations to aid Poland.

3. After presenting a two-hour ultimatum to Germany, Britain declares war at 11 A.M. and France declares war at 5 P.M. Winston Churchill joins the Cabinet as First Lord of the Admiralty and Anthony Eden becomes Secretary of State for the Dominions.

8. President Roosevelt proclaims a national emergency "to the extent necessary for the proper observance, safeguarding and enforcing of the neutrality of the United States and the strengthening of our national defense within the limits of peacetime authorizations."

15. The Soviet Union and Japan agree to an armistice on the Far Eastern Front.

28. Molotov and Ribbentrop sign an agreement in Moscow partitioning Poland.

October 6. Following the victory over Poland, Hitler makes his "last peace offer" to the Allies.

19. Britain, France, and Turkey sign a mutual-assistance pact with proviso that Turkey shall not be compelled to fight Russia.

November 4. President Roosevelt signs the amended Neutrality Act, lifting the arms embargo but adding the cash-and-carry clause. American shipping is forbidden to enter the war zones.

28. The Soviet Union denounces its nonaggression pact with Finland and two days later Soviet troops invade Finland while Soviet airplanes bomb Finnish cities.

December 17. On orders from Berlin, the German pocket battleship, *Graf Spee*, is scuttled by its crew outside Montevideo.

January 26. Russian troops begin to crack Finland's Mannerheim Line.

February 12. The first Australian and New Zealand troops arrive at Suez.

March 12. Russia and Finland sign an armistice which cedes western Finland to the Soviet Union.

19. Paul Reynaud forms a new French Cabinet to replace that of Daladier, receiving a majority of one vote.

April 7. The Allies warn that they are mining the waters off Norway. Norway and Holland protest this as violation of international law.

9. German troops occupy Denmark without resistance and land in Norway at Narvik and Oslo.

May 3. Colonel O. B. Getz, Norwegian commander, asks for armistice and peace negotiations with Germany as British withdrawal continues.

8. Chamberlain's majority in House of Commons falls to 81 as 130 Conservatives abstain from giving government a vote of confidence.

10. German troops invade Holland, Belgium, and Luxembourg. The British Army moves into northern Belgium. Chamberlain resigns as British Prime Minister and King George VI asks Winston Churchill to form a new government.

11. Churchill forms a new Cabinet, retaining Halifax and Chamberlain, but adding three Laborites who had hitherto refused to hold office. Foreign Minister Arita of Japan announces that his country will not permit the Netherlands Indies to change hands.

14. Holland capitulates to Germany.

16. German troops pass Sedan, thereby in effect sealing the doom of France.

18. Premier Reynaud appoints Marshal Pétain Vice-Premier.

19. General Weygand succeeds General Gamelin as French chief of staff.

20. British troops begin evacuating Belgian ports.

22. British Parliament passes the Emergency Powers Defense Act giving the Churchill government unlimited wartime powers.

28. King Leopold of Belgium surrenders his army of 500,000 to the Germans.

29. Large-scale British evacuation of Dunkirk begins.

June 4. The British evacuation of Dunkirk completed with 335,000 men saved and more than 30,000 casualties.

10. Foreign Minister Ciano announces that Italy will consider itself at war with France and Britain. President Roosevelt says, "The hand that held the dagger has stuck it into the back of its neighbor."

14. German troops occupy Paris which the French had announced was an open city and would not be defended.

16. Premier Reynaud resigns and is succeeded by Marshal Pétain.

17. Marshal Pétain sues for peace.

22. French delegation signs armistice with Germany.

29. In response to Russian demands, Rumania cedes Bessarabia and northern Bukovina to the Soviet Union.

July 3. Great Britain takes over all French war vessels in British ports and disables part of the French fleet at Oran after the French commander refuses to accept a British ultimatum.

4. Rumania establishes a pro-German Cabinet.

5. The Pétain government breaks off diplomatic relations with Britain.

12. The British agree to close for three months the Burma Road to armament traffic destined for China.

August 16. After several weeks of increased air activity, the British repulse wave after wave of German war planes, inflicting 217 enemy losses in three days.

22. German planes launch first mass night attack on London.

31. Rumania cedes two thirds of Transylvania to Hungary.

September 3. The United States transfers fifty overage destroyers to Great Britain in exchange for ninety-nine year leases to naval and aircraft bases in the Atlantic.

6. King Carol of Rumania abdicates.

8. Marshal Goering takes command of air attacks on Britain.

15. German air attacks on London reach their peak as RAF destroys 185 German fighting craft.

23. General de Gaulle and Free French forces, supported by British war vessels, withdraw from Dakar after failing to persuade local representatives of the Pétain regime to surrender.

27. Germany, Italy, and Japan sign a ten-year mutual-assistance pact.

October 27. Italian war planes and troops attack Greece from Albania, following Greek rejection of a three-hour Italian ultimatum.

November 12. British aircraft seriously damage several large Italian war vessels in Taranto harbor.

13. Soviet Foreign Commissar Molotov visits Berlin.

16. German planes launch mass night attack on city of Coventry. Italians begin to evacuate their Albanian base at Koritza.

December 6. Greeks capture Porto Edda and Marshal Badoglio resigns as Italian chief of staff.

10. British launch offensive against Italian troops in Libya and Egypt.

15. British drive all Italians from Egypt and pursue them into Libya.

23. Lord Halifax appointed British Ambassador to the United States to replace Lord Lothian who died on December 12.

1941

January 26. British troops capture Tobruk.

February 6. British troops capture Benghazi.

10. Britain severs diplomatic relations with Rumania.

March 2. Bulgaria joins the Axis.

11. President Roosevelt signs the Lease-Lend Act.

April 3. Axis land forces open drive on British troops in Libya.

6. German troops invade Yugoslavia.

13. The Soviet Union and Japan sign a neutrality and nonaggression pact.

14. Axis drive against British North African forces penetrates Egypt.

19. Pro-Axis Premier of Irak begins a series of uprisings which the British finally crush on May 31.

27. German troops enter Athens.

May 10. Rudolf Hess, Hitler's deputy and number three man in the Nazi hierarchy, flies to Great Britain and lands on the estate of the Duke of Hamilton. German air attacks on British cities suddenly cease.

20. Main Italian forces begin withdrawal from Ethiopia and surrender the country to Britain on June 1.

27. President Roosevelt proclaims an unlimited national emergency.

June 1. British evacuation of Crete is completed.

8. British and Free French forces invade Syria.

18. Turkey and Germany sign a trade treaty and nonaggression pact.

22. German troops, together with Finns and Rumanians, invade Russia.

23. Red Air Force raids East Prussia.

27. Red Air Force bombs Finland and Rumania, while Red Navy shells Constanta, Rumanian Black Sea port.

29. German High Command claims the capture of Minsk, capital of White Russia.

30. Defense Committee of five, headed by Stalin, is formed, to take over all authority in Russia.

July 3. The ten-day battle of Bialystok ends, Germany claiming to have captured 100,000 prisoners. Russians claim to have killed, wounded, or captured 700,-000 Germans in the Minsk area.

7. United States troops announce the occupation of Iceland.

11. Red armies put under the command of Marshals Voroshilov, Timoshenko, **and Budenny.**

12. British and Free French troops complete the conquest of Syria.

14. Russians announce the sinking of thirteen German troop ships, two destroyers, a bargeload of tanks, and the firing of thirteen other troop ships, in the Baltic.

16. German High Command announces the capture of Smolensk, 230 miles west of Moscow, and the complete shattering of the Stalin Line.

22. Moscow bombed by German planes for the first time.

25. President Roosevelt freezes Japanese assets; Britain follows suit the next day.

27. German spearhead reported within forty-three miles of Leningrad. Finns claim to have recaptured all territory ceded to Russia at the end of the

31. Russo-Finnish War.
First Italian troops arrive at the Russian front.

August 14. President Roosevelt and Prime Minister Churchill issue their eight-point peace aims, following Atlantic Charter conference.

17. Germans capture the naval base of Nikolaev, claiming seizure of a battleship, a cruiser, four destroyers, and two submarines.

21. Marshal Voroshilov calls on people to organize civilian defense groups and

fight to the end to save Leningrad. German forces are within sixty miles of the city.

26. Berlin reports capture of Dniepropetrovsk.

28. Moscow announces that the Cooper Dam, one of the largest in the world, had been destroyed to prevent the Germans from utilizing it. Germans capture Tallinn, capital of Estonia.

28. Iran ends resistance to occupation by Anglo-Soviet forces.

30. Finnish High Command announces capture of Viborg, which the Russians had laid waste before withdrawing.

September 1. Red Air Force raids Berlin, Königsberg, Danzig, and Memel.

7. Soviet Supreme Council orders the removal of the German population of the Volga region to Siberia and Kazakstan.

8. Germans claim to have cut off all land communication with Leningrad, having captured Schlüsselberg, railroad center on Lake Ladoga.

11. President Roosevelt orders American war vessels to shoot first at Axis warships in waters vital to the defense of the United States.

14. German forces advance to within fifteen miles of Leningrad.

17. Germans begin their drive on the Crimea.

18. Russia orders the conscription of every man between the ages of sixteen and fifty for military training after working hours. Red Army defenders of Leningrad hurl Germans back ten miles and recapture three villages near the city.

19. German High Command announces the capture of Kiev, ancient capital of the Ukraine.

21. German forces reach the Sea of Azov, Berlin announces.

22. Red Army claims destruction of six German infantry battalions in the Ukraine.

24. German army reaches the suburbs of Leningrad.

30. Russians evacuate Poltava.

October 2. Hitler announces the beginning of the "last great decisive battle" against Russia.

7. Berlin claims capture of Mariupol and Ossipenko on the Sea of Azov.

8. Orel captured by the Germans.

9. Dietrich, Reich press chief, reports: "Soviet Russia is done with."

13. Red Army abandons Vyazma, 125 miles west of Moscow.

15. Red Army withdraws from Kalinin, 100 miles northwest of Moscow.

16. Odessa taken by German and Rumanian troops after a two-month siege.

17. United States Navy announces the torpedoing of the destroyer *Kearny* on the Iceland patrol.

19. Stalin proclaims Moscow in a state of siege. Germans claim capture of Taganrog, forty miles from Rostov.

22. Snowstorms slow up German drive on Moscow.

23. General Zhukov, Chief of General Staff, replaces Timoshenko as commander of central front.

24. German High Command announces capture of Kharkhov.

26. Red Army evacuates Stalino, in the Donets basin.

30. Germans advance to within seventy miles of Moscow in the south and to within sixty-five miles in the southwest, at Malo Yaroslavets.

31. Germans claim capture of Kalinin.

November 2. German High Command announces capture of Simferopol, capital of the Crimea.

4. Germans report capture of Theodosia, on the Black Sea.

6. Stalin reports German losses at 4,500,000 men killed, wounded, or captured since the beginning of war; Russian losses, 378,000 missing, 350,000 killed, and 1,020,000 wounded. Germany reports Russian losses at from seven to eight million men killed, wounded, or captured.

6. Soviet government announces appointment of Maxim Litvinov as Ambassador to the United States.

12. Red Army pushes Germans back five miles at Tula.

16. Germans claim capture of Kerch, in the Crimea.

22. German High Command reports capture of Rostov on the Don.

26. Germans advance to within twenty-five miles of Moscow on the northwest.

29. Red Army recaptures Rostov, annihilating five German divisions; Germans retreating toward Taganrog.

December 7. Japan attacks Malaya, Hong Kong, Guam, the Philippine Islands, Wake Island, and Hawaii.

8. The United States declares war on Japan.

11. The United States declares war on Germany and Italy, following war declarations by the German and Italian governments. General Field Marshal von Bock, commander of German forces on the central front, relieved of his command.

16. Red Army recaptures Klin, fifty-one miles northwest of Moscow, and continues advance in the Crimea.

21. Red Army recaptures Volokolamsk, forty miles from Moscow. General Field Marshal von Brauchitsch removed from command of German armies, Hitler taking over.

22. Prime Minister Churchill arrives in Washington for war conferences with President Roosevelt.

24. Red Army drives Germans to Orel.

31. Red Army recaptures Kerch and Theodosia, in the Crimea.

1942

January 1. Twenty-six United Nations pledge all resources for victory and agree not to sign a separate peace.

1. Red Army retakes Kaluga.

6. Red Army recaptures almost the entire Kerch Peninsula.

12. Soviet troops command entrance to Petsamo, important ice-free port in Finland.

20. Mozhaisk falls to the Red Army after eighteen days of resistance.

24. Red Army advances seventy-five miles in reaching Kholm and recovers 2000 towns and villages.

26. American Expeditionary Force lands in Northern Ireland.

February 9. Red Army gains in the Donets and pushes back encircling armies at Leningrad.

15. Singapore surrenders to the Japanese.

19. Sir Stafford Cripps enters the British War Cabinet as Lord Privy Seal and Leader of the House of Commons.

25. Red High Command reports capture of Staraya Russia after encirclement and defeat of German Sixteenth Army.

March 7. Moscow announces that 200,000 Germans are trapped in the Staraya Russia area.

17. General MacArthur arrives in Australia to assume supreme command of United Nations forces in the southwest Pacific.

23. Red Army takes posts on Kalinin front despite stiffening German resistance.

28. Red troops, by sea and air, attack German lines in Murmansk area and deal smashing blow to German and Finnish troops.

30. Kharkhov is encircled by advancing Red Army troops.

April 7. Red High Command reports that Air Force and ground batteries destroyed 415 German planes during the previous eight days, with a Russian loss of 84.

16. Moscow radio reports that one Soviet guard division killed over 25,000 Germans, captured 200 populated places, and disabled 100 tanks and armored cars.

18. Total mobilization of Russia's 193 million people against anticipated German spring offensive was ordered, mustering all for industrial and farm production. Red Air Force, using seventy planes, bombs Vardoe in northern Norway.

21. Moscow radio reports 1500 German planes destroyed in six weeks ending April 14.

29. *Komsomolskaya Pravda* asserts that the Red Army, during the winter campaign, drove Germans from 11,000 inhabited points, including 60 cities.

May 11. Germans begin huge offensive in the Crimea.

12. Red Army, directed by Marshal Timoshenko, begin powerful drive on Kharkov.

16. German High Command claims recapture of Kerch, in the Crimea.

June 11. Foreign Commissar Molotov's presence in Washington announced. For a week, he and President Roosevelt planned new war action and Roosevelt acknowledged urgent need for Second Front in 1942.

21. General Rommel's Afrika Korps captures Tobruk and 25,000 Allied soldiers.

30. Allied lines in Egypt stiffen as Rommel drives to within 100 miles of Alexandria.

July 1. Germans capture Crimean city of Sevastopol.

27. Germans capture Rostov in million-man offensive against Caucasus.

August 7. United States Marines land on Guadalcanal.

9. British imprison Gandhi and other Indian Nationalists who launch civil dis-obedience campaign for independence.

19. British and Canadian troops raid Channel port of Dieppe with heavy losses.

September 21. German offensive in south Russia reaches suburbs of Stalingrad.

October 20. Russians throw back German attack on Stalingrad.

25. General Montgomery's British 8th Army checks German advance at El Alamein.

November 4. General Montgomery opens offensive against Rommel's desert army in Egypt.

7. Allied troops under General Eisenhower land successfully near Casablanca, Oran, and Algiers.

8. Marshal Pétain's Vichy government breaks relations with the United States.

12. Admiral Darlan, Vichy commander of all French North African forces, orders resistance to end. German armies enter unoccupied France.

13. British 8th Army recaptures Tobruk.

15. Admiral Darlan appoints General Giraud top French commander in North Africa.

27. French scuttle bulk of their Navy at Toulon.

December 3. Germans abandon fight for Stalingrad as Russian counter-offensive begins.

24. Admiral Darlan assassinated at Algiers.

1943

January 14. President Roosevelt arrives at Casablanca and holds "unconditional sur-render" conference with Prime Minister Churchill.

27. Germans establish new lines west of Stalingrad as Russian counter-offensive gains ground along the whole eastern front.

February 9. Japanese abandon whole Guadalcanal area in the Solomon Islands.

16. Russian armies recapture Kharkhov in 375-mile advance from Stalingrad.

25. American troops recover from their first set back in North Africa at Kasserine Pass.

March 16. Russians evacuate Kharkhov as Germans start new offensive.

23. British 8th Army breaks Mareth Line in Tunisia.

April 26. Russia breaks off relations with Polish Exile government which had urged investigation of German charges that Russians had killed 10,000 Polish officers near Katyn forest.

May 7. American troops take Bizerte; British enter Tunis.

11. Prime Minister Churchill arrives for new conferences in Washington.

21. Marshal Stalin announces liquidation of Third Communist International.

June 11. The Italian island of Pantelleria surrenders to Allies.

July 10. Allied troops under General Eisenhower land in Sicily.

25. Mussolini resigns and Marshal Badoglio takes over.

August 17. President Roosevelt and Prime Minister Churchill confer at Quebec on Second Front in 1944.

September 3. Allied troops cross Messina Straits and land in Italy.

8. Italian government accepts Allied surrender terms.

9. American Fifth Army lands at Salerno.

11. Troops under General MacArthur capture New Guinea port of Salamaua.

26. Russian armies take Smolensk on central front.

October 1. Allied troops take Naples.

13. Italy declares war on Germany.

19. Big Three Foreign Ministers meet at Moscow.

November 6. Russian troops take Kiev.

20. United States Marines land on Tarawa in the Gilbert Islands.

22. Roosevelt, Churchill, and Chiang Kai-shek meet at Cairo and draw up war aims declaration pledging themselves to strip Japan of all conquests achieved "by fraud and by force."

December 4. Roosevelt, Churchill, and Stalin wind up the meetings at Teheran with a statement pledging full cooperation in war against Germany.

24. General Eisenhower appointed Supreme Allied Commander for invasion of Europe from the west.

1944

January 11. Russian troops cross pre-war Polish border and Soviet government announces that Western Ukraine and White Russia will be incorporated into Soviet Union.

22. Allied troops land near Anzio, 30 miles below Rome.

February 6. German troops counterattack at Cassino. Allied forces fail to advance at Anzio.

March 4. Russian Armies under Marshal Zhukov open new offensive, advancing 31 miles into Poland.

6. Flying fortresses drop 2,000 tons of explosives in first big daylight raid on Berlin.

20. Russian troops cross Dniester River into Rumania.

22. Japanese troops penetrate western India, striking up from Burma.

April 22. American troops under General MacArthur land at Hollandia in Dutch New Guinea.

25. Japanese open offensive designed to cut across south China.

30. American and British air forces announce they dropped record tonnage of 80,000 tons of bombs on enemy territories during month of April.

May 10. Russians recapture Sevastopol.

12. Allies resume offensive against Germans in central Italy.

25. Two Allied offensives, one from Anzio and the other from Cassino, make contact and establish single line south of Rome.

June 4. Germans abandon Rome to the Allies.

6. Allied troops under command of General Eisenhower begin landings in Normandy.

9. Ivanoe Bonomi replaces Marshal Badoglio as Italian Prime Minister.

16. American superfortresses attack southern Japan.

19. First V-1 Flying bombs fall on England as Allied troops continue to widen their bridgeheads in Normandy.

20. Admiral Nimitz announces big naval victory as Americans invade Marianas and Japanese lose 14 war vessels.

25. American troops enter Cherbourg.

28. General Montgomery opens offensive against Caen at eastern end of Normandy beachhead.

30. American airmen abandon Chinese base of Hengyang as Japanese advance continues.

July 3. Russians take Minsk on central front.

12. Russian Armies threaten East Prussia.

18. British break Germans lines at Caen; Americans break through at St. Lô.

19. Japanese Cabinet of General Tojo resigns and is succeeded by General Koiso.

20. German Army officers fail in bomb attempt on Hitler.

21. Russians announce creation of a Polish Committee of National Liberation as they prepare to take Lwow.

25. American troops under General Bradley start drive across France.

27. Heinrich Himmler becomes dictator of German home front.

August 2. Russian troops reach Baltic, and President Ryti of Finland resigns. Marshal Mannerheim takes over.

7. American and British troops overrun entire Breton peninsula.

15. Allied troops land in southern France.

17. General Patton's armored troops drive to within 40 miles of Paris.

24. Rumania surrenders. Allied troops and French resistance fighters take Bordeaux.

25. German commandant in Paris surrenders to French General LeClerc.

28. General Patton's troops cross the Marne.

31. All German fronts in the Balkans collapse. British enter Amiens. Germans retreat in southern France. Americans reach Maginot Line.

September 4. British take Brussels and enter Antwerp.

5. Finnish-Russian armistice signed. Russia declares war on Bulgaria and Bulgaria surrenders.

12. American troops cross German border near Trier; Russian patrols enter East Prussia.

17. Allied airborne troops land inside Holland, but fail to make junction with land forces.

October 3. Polish patriots in Warsaw surrender to Germans as Russians accuse them of disobeying orders.

9. British, Russian, Chinese, and American delegates conclude Dumbarton Oaks Conference and draw up first blue-print for world security league.

14. British and Greek troops enter Athens.

19. American troops land at Leyte in the central Philippines.

26. Three day naval battle in Leyte Gulf cripples Japanese Navy.

28. General Stilwell recalled from China to the United States.

November 7. President Roosevelt re-elected for fourth term.

24. Superfortresses based on Saipan bomb Tokyo.

December 3. Greek leftists refuse to surrender arms to British and civil war begins.

16. Germans launch counter-offensive in Ardennes Forest.

24. Allied air and ground attacks check German counter-offensive.

25. Churchill and Eden arrive in Athens.

31. Pro-Russian Poles set up new regime in Lublin and break off with Polish exiled regime in London.

1945

January 9. American troops land on main Philippine Island of Luzon.

12. Russian winter offensive drives north and south of Warsaw.

17. Russians capture Warsaw.

February 5. American troops enter Manila.

7. Roosevelt, Churchill, and Stalin conclude Yalta Conference on occupation of Germany and liberation of Europe.

19. United States Marines land on Iwo Jima Island.

March 7. United States troops cross Rhine at Remagen Bridge.

26. Allied troops complete conquest of east bank of Rhine.

27. General Patton's Army takes Frankfurt and Argentina declares war on Axis.

April 1. American troops land on Okinawa.

5. Prime Minister Koiso and entire Japanese Cabinet resign and are succeeded by Admiral Suzuki. Russia denounces neutrality pact with Japan.

9. Russian troops enter Vienna and Koenigsberg. Allied troops reach River Elbe.

12. President Roosevelt dies.

22. Russian troops enter Berlin. Allied offensive in Italy sweeps through Bologna.

25. United Nations Conference at San Francisco begins.

26. Italian Anti-Fascists kill Mussolini.

May 1. German radio announces death of Hitler in Berlin.

2. Russians take Berlin. German Armies in Italy surrender.

6. Admiral Doenitz, successor to Hitler, orders all German armed forces to surrender. General Jodl surrenders at Reims to General Eisenhower.

8. Britain and America celebrate VE Day.

9. Russians celebrate VE Day. Marshal Keitel surrenders in Berlin to Marshal Zhukov.

23. Prime Minister Churchill resigns and sets British general election for July 5.

June 5. British, French, Russian, and American commanders issue four-power declaration from Berlin proclaiming Germany's complete defeat and their assumption of supreme authority.

21. American troops complete conquest of Okinawa.

26. Fifty United Nations sign World Security Charter at San Francisco.

July 3. Tokyo radio reports 5,000,000 casualties in American air raids.

17. Truman, Churchill, and Stalin meet at Potsdam to draw up final terms of

German settlement and make other post-war arrangements.

26. Britain, China, and America issue "Potsdam Declaration" outlining unconditional surrender terms to Japan. British elections show big Labor victory and Attlee returns to Potsdam to replace Churchill.

29. Japanese reject Potsdam ultimatum.

31. American air commanders announce that eight more Japanese cities face destruction.

August 6. President Truman announces that first atomic bomb has obliterated Hiroshima.

8. Soviet Union declares war on Japan and Russian Armies advance into Manchuria.

9. American planes drop second atomic bomb on Nagasaki. Russian advances continue.

10. Japanese ask for peace provided Emperor retains his powers.

11. Allies reply that Japanese Emperor must accept orders from them.

14. Japanese Government accepts Allied peace terms which Russians endorse.

27. Third U. S. Fleet enters Tokyo Bay.

28. First American troops land on Japanese soil.

September 2. Japanese officials sign unconditional surrender documents in presence of Allied commanders on the U.S.S. *Missouri*.

ABOUT THE AUTHOR

David Low got his start as a political cartoonist shortly after the turn of the century when, at the age of eleven, he began drawing for The Spectator *in his native city of Christchurch, New Zealand. At the age of twenty, he moved to Sydney, Australia, where he worked for the* Bulletin, *and then journeyed to London to join the staff of the* Star. *Since 1927, David Low has drawn regularly for the* Evening Standard *of London. Lord Beaverbrook, the proprietor of that paper, has often disagreed with the political views of his chief cartoonist to whom, however, he has always given a completely free rein. Many collections of Low cartoons have appeared in Great Britain. This is his third to appear in the United States. His work is also familiar to readers of* The Nation *and* The New York Times.